David D. Demarest

The Reformed Church in America

Its origin, development and characteristics. Fourth Edition

David D. Demarest

The Reformed Church in America
Its origin, development and characteristics. Fourth Edition

ISBN/EAN: 9783337295912

Printed in Europe, USA, Canada, Australia, Japan

Cover: Foto ©Lupo / pixelio.de

More available books at **www.hansebooks.com**

Nisi Dominus Frustra

Eendracht maakt Macht

THE REFORMED CHURCH IN AMERICA.

ITS ORIGIN,

DEVELOPMENT AND CHARACTERISTICS.

BY

DAVID D. DEMAREST, D. D.,

PROFESSOR OF PASTORAL THEOLOGY AND SACRED RHETORIC
IN THE THEOLOGICAL SEMINARY AT
NEW BRUNSWICK, N. J.

FOURTH EDITION.

REVISED AND ENLARGED.

NEW YORK:
BOARD OF PUBLICATION
OF THE
REFORMED CHURCH IN AMERICA.
1889.

PREFACE.

In the winter of 1853-4, I delivered a course of lectures on the History and Characteristics of the Reformed Protestant Dutch Church to the people of my charge, in the City of Hudson, New York. These lectures were afterwards, by invitation, repeated in the Reformed Dutch church, in Wayne Street, Jersey City, and in the Second Reformed Dutch Church of New Brunswick. Their publication was advised and asked for by many on the ground that there was a want of, and desire for, a volume which should present in a compact and accessible form, the history and peculiarities of this Church, to be circulated among its families, placed in the Sunday school libraries, and put into the hands of all who might desire the information which such a book ought to contain. The Board of Publication issued the work in the year 1856.

Three editions have been published, but for many years the book has been out of print, and rarely has one who desired a copy been able to obtain it. The facts that thirty-five years of history have been made since the book was written; that many matters of interest then unknown, have since come to light; and that there is now a great and daily increasing interest in the civil and ecclesiastical history of the Netherlands, as well as in the early history of our Church in this country, have induced me to comply with the request of the Board of Publication to prepare a new edition, in which the history should be brought down to the present time. The work has been entirely rewritten, though the general plan has been retained and the materials have been arranged in the same number of chapters. The title of the book and the headings of the chapters have been somewhat changed.

Inasmuch as the rise of the Church in the Netherlands was very closely connected with the civil history of that country, the first two chapters seemed to be necessary to a clear understanding of the ecclesiastical history. In fact, no one can understand the latter without reading the works of Schiller, Davies, Prescott and Motley, or, if possible, consulting the sources from which these writers have drawn. Our readers will also do well to consult the admirable volume on the Reformed Church in the Netherlands by the Rev. M. G. Hansen, which has been published by the Board of Publication. Also, one who would more fully inform himself about the early history of the Church in this country, will read Brodhead's History of New York, Mrs. Lamb's History of the City of New York, Gunn's Life of Livingston, and local histories and pamphlets which are too numerous to be mentioned. Above all, he cannot pass by Corwin's Manual of the Reformed Church in America, the volume of Centennial Discourses published in 1874, and the Centennial Volume of the Theological Seminary at New Brunswick, published in 1885.

Besides these, the following are some of the works that have been consulted in preparing this volume.

Acta Synodi Nationalis, 1620.

Acts and Proceedings of the General Synod of the Reformed Church in America, 16 vols.

Altingii Historia de Ecclesiis Palatinis, 1728.

Brandt's Historie der Reformatie, Amsterdam, 1671.

Calder's Memoirs of Episcopius, New York, 1837.

Coetus and Conferentie journals and pamphlets.

D alton's Johannes á Lasco, Gotha, 1881.

Ens, J. Kort Historisch Berigt van de publieke Schriften, Utrecht, 1733.

Glasius, B., Geschiedenis de Nat. Syn. Dordrecht, 1860.

'sGravesande 200 jaarige Gedachtenis van het Eerste Synode Neder. Kercken, 1769.

Kerkelijke Handboekje, Delft, 1738.

á Lasco, Opera, Ed. Kuyper, Amsterdam, 1866.

Le Long, I., Kort Historisch Verhaal van de Eersten Oorsprong der Ned. Geref. Kerken onder 't Cruis, Amsterdam, 1751.

Manual of Missions, New York, 1877.

Mensinga, J. A. M., Verhandeling over de Liturgische Schriften der Ned. Hervormde Kerk, 'sGravenhage, 1851.

Post-Acta of the Synod of Dort, Rotterdam, 1732.

Pijper's, Jan Uytenhove, Leiden, 1883.

Schriften der Remonstranten en Contra-remonstranten, 12 vols., 1618.

Scott's, T., Synod of Dort, Utica, 1831.

Van Iperen, J., Kerkelijk Historie van het Psalm-gezang, 1777.

Van Toorenenbergen, J. J., Eene Bladzijde uit de Geschiedenis der Nederlandsche Geloofsbelijdenis, 'sGravenhage, 1861.

Vinke, H. E., Libri Symbolici Ecclesiæ Reform. Nederland. Utrecht, 1846.

The writer acknowledges his indebtedness to Mr. John S. Bussing for the use of his dies for printing the illuminated emblem or frontispiece, and for his careful and interesting description of it; to the Rev. Dr. J. H. Good, of Philadelphia, for the use of the electrotype plate of the "Synod of Dort," and to the Rev. Dr. E. T. Corwin for valuable help in preparing the work for the press.

This book is one of outlines, and brevity has been

constantly studied at the sacrifice of very interesting
matter. It is hoped that the little volume will awaken the
gratitude of our people for God's gracious dealings with
this ancient Church; will cause them to prize their
heritage and to honor the memories of those who at great
cost procured and transmitted it; and will stimulate
them to imitation of their loyalty to the Head of the
Church, and of devotion to this branch of it, in which,
God has by His good Providence placed them.

New Brunswick.
        June 26th, 1889.

CONTENTS.

I. ORIGIN.

I.

II. DEVELOPMENT.

IV.

V.

III. CHARACTERISTICS.

VI.

VII.

VIII.

IX.

THE HISTORY

OF THE

COAT-OF-ARMS.

BY JOHN S. BUSSING

It has been the custom during many centuries, for families, churches and states, to make use of certain emblematic devices by which they are recognized among themselves, and by the rest of the world.

These emblems were first displayed on seals, medals, banners, etc., and in the times of the Crusaders, were used as badges of honor. They consisted of shield and crest, with supporters and mottoes often added. These symbols have a value from the incidents which led to their adoption, and are calculated to awaken sentiments of respect among all who consider their derivation and their meaning.

One of the many historic reminders of the fathers in Holland, of which the Reformed Church in America is proud, is the coat-of-arms of William of Orange. In 1568, "William the Silent," Prince of Orange, led the cause of the Reformation against the Pope and Philip II., and when, in 1579, the Union of Utrecht was consummated, the "Republic of the Seven United Provinces in Holland," was formed, and William of Orange was invited to become its leader. Holland, under him, finally gained her freedom, and the churches had rest from persecution. It was therefore only natural that those connected with the Dutch Church in America should select as their escutcheon, a shield used by one who had done so much for the country and church of their forefathers.

The earliest record of the shield of Orange and Nassau, is found in the Medallic History of the Netherlands, published in Amsterdam, 1690, by Gerard Van Loon. On a medal which was struck by Charles V., in 1556, when William of Orange was installed in the Order of the Golden Fleece, there is embellished the arms of the Prince. In 1568, another medal, oval in form, appeared, which also bears his arms. In 1607, a medal was struck on the occasion of the marriage of his eldest son. On this his arms again appear.

Visitors to the tomb of "William the Silent" in the cathedral at Delft, Holland, may see this shield cut in marble and beautifully illuminated.

It is also interesting to note that in the Art Museum in Cincinnati, there is a Dutch silver collar of the seventeenth century; a copy of one in the Royal Museum at the Hague, on which is engraved the shield with all the quarterings exactly as we have them on our emblem.

The first appearance of this coat-of-arms in this country, as far as can at present be ascertained, was on the fly-leaf of the "Magazine of the Reformed Dutch Church," which was issued in the year 1826. From what source that imprint was copied cannot be ascertained, as no reference is made to it in any of the volumes of the magazine. It was from a plain wood cut, but well executed for that time. The engraver appears to have made an error in placing the lions in the fourth quarter of the large shield, for every authority gives them as *passant* and not *rampant*. The pillars which support the shield, must have been added at the time that this began to be used as an ecclesiastical emblem, for no mention of them is made in any of the ancient records. It may be that the spires which surmount the pillars and point to the stars, were intended to be emblematic of the church pointing heavenward. The crown, crest and mantle were rudely depicted in the cut with which we have all become familiar. As they here appear they conform more closely to the original. Both the mottoes are now placed on ribbons, one above and the other below; originally they did not belong to the coat-of-arms, but as they have been so long associated with it they have properly become a part of our emblem.

In the year 1839 the Christian Intelligencer placed the emblem which the magazine had used, at the head of its columns, where it has remained ever since, and it is probable that all the dies now in use are copies of one of these. Within the last ten years it has come into general use in many of our churches and Sunday schools, being printed on the orders of services at the Christmas and Easter Festivals, and in some cases it has been engraved on gold medals. Several churches have already given it a place of honor; some on stained glass windows, others on banners and tablets. Among them may be mentioned churches in the following places, viz.: Albany, Syracuse, Schenectady, Athens, Catskill, Port Jervis, Hackensack, Newark.

The following detailed description of the coat-of-arms was mainly taken from the "Centennial of the Theological Seminary of the Reformed Church in America, 1784-1884."

The various armorial bearings on the shields, originate from the fact that the Princes of Orange were also lords of other principalities, all of which are represented in this emblem.

The first quarter of the *large shield* bears the arms of Nassau, the capital of which was the birthplace of. William the Silent. It has a gold lion rampant, on a blue field, surrounded by seventeen gold billets repre-

senting, it is said, the union of the ten states of the
Netherlands with the seven states of Holland under
William. The second quarter represents Katzenelnbo-
gen and has a red lion rampant gardant, crowned, on a
gold field. The third quarter represents Vianden and
has a red field banded with silver. The fourth quarter
has two gold lions passant gardant, on a red field, and
is the shield of Dietz.

The *small shield* is also quartered. The first and
fourth quarters bearing diagonal bands of gold on a red
shield represent the principalities of Chalons. The
second and third quarters, with a blue horn or bugle
suspended by a red ribbon on a gold field, that of
Orange. These martial horns symbolize the courageous
leadership of those who took up arms against the Moors
and Saracens.

The *smallest shield* is that of Jane of Geneva, who
married one of the Princes of Orange. It is divided into
nine squares or panels, five of which have gold, and
four blue fields.

The *crown* which surmounts the shield represents the
Emperor, Charles the Great, who, while sovereign of
the Netherlands, granted them imperial privileges, as
also the right of carrying the imperial crown above the
coat-of-arms.

On a coin issued at Ghent in 1582, appears the motto
Nisi Dominus Frustra—" Without the Lord all is vain."
The Dutch had to struggle for a home and a church,
and the motto fitly expresses their deep religious convictions, and their sincere hope in God.

The motto in Dutch—*Eendracht maakt macht*—signifies, " Union makes strength." It is a free translation of
the Latin motto of the " Republic of the Seven United
Provinces of Holland," and was the rallying cry in times
of despondency.

"The genuineness of these heraldic devices, the stirring historical associations connected with the shield of William, the exalted character of its owner, that great leader who was one of the founders alike of the Dutch Republic and the Reformed Church, and the motto so full of earnest inspiration, justify the ready acceptance and sustained popularity of this, the best known graphic symbol of the Reformed Church in America."

GUIDE FOR ILLUMINATING.

It is a rule in Heraldry that certain lines indicate certain colors. One may therefore readily know what color to employ in illuminating, by observing the following:—perpendicular lines indicate red; horizontal lines, blue; dots, gold; a plain surface, silver.

The coloring of the ribbons is optional, but the coloring of the shield and crest must conform to given rules. The use of the red ribbon at the top, and the blue at the bottom of our emblem, has become so general, that these color lines are inserted in this new die

---

NOTE.—From the Medallic History of Holland, above referred to, and other sources, Rev. Dr. H. C. McCook prepared his historical decorations for the Council of the Reformed Churches, holding the Presbyterian order, which met in Philadelphia, in 1880. Subsequently Rev. Dr. P. D. Van Cleef prepared his description of these armorial devices for the Centennial Volume of the New Brunswick Seminary, 1884. See Medallische Historie der Republic von Holland. A copy, in French, is in the Philadelphia Library; and a copy, in Dutch, is owned by the Hon. Garret D. W. Vroom, of Trenton, N. J. See, also Dr. McCook's Souvenir of the Historical decorations, 1880; and Centennial of the Theological Seminary at New Brunswick, 1884.   D. D. D.

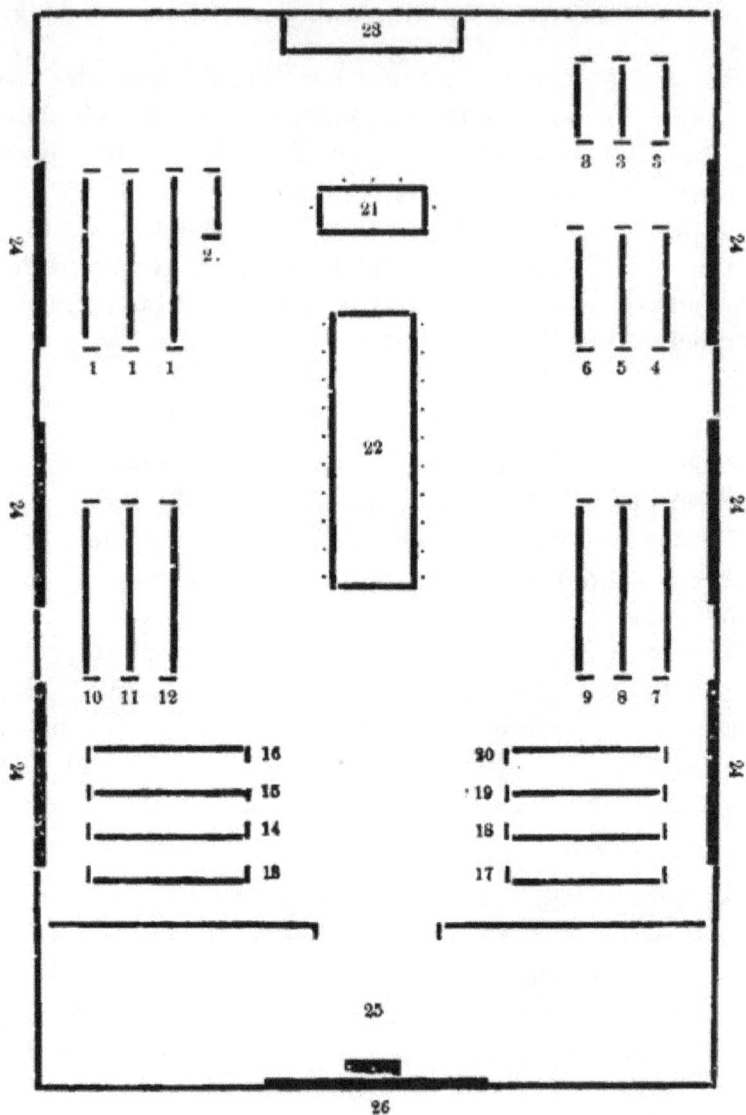

KEY TO THE SYNOD OF DORT.

THE SYNOD OF DORT.

The President is seated at the small table in the centre. The German Delegates are
on the side seats to the right.

In the following explanation, the figures in brackets indicate the number, in each case, of the persons who signed the proceedings of the Synod at its close :

1. The political deputies (15).
2. Their secretary.
3. The English theologians (5).
4. The theologians from the Palatinate (3).
5. The delegates from Hesse Cassel (4).
6. The Swiss theologians (5).
7. The Wedderaw correspondents (2).
8. The theologians from Geneva (2).
9. The theologians from Bremen (3) and Embden (2).
10. The Netherlands Professors.
11. Deputies from Gelderland and Zutphen (4).
12. Deputies from South Holland (5).
13. Deputies from North Holland (5).
14. Deputies from Zeeland (5).
15. Deputies from Utrecht (2).
16. Deputies from Friesland (4).
17. Deputies from Over-Yssel (6).
18. Deputies from Groningen (6).
19. Deputies from Drenthe (2).
20. Delegates from Walloon Churches (6).
21. The President, Adsessors, and Scribes (5).
22. Remonstrant Professors and Ministers who had been cited to appear before the Synod.
23. The fire-place, having a large fire burning in it.
24. Windows.
25. Standing-space for spectators.
26. The door.

CHAPTER I.

The Reformed Church of the Netherlands, mother of
the Reformed Church in America, was born amid the
storms of political revolution, and was trained in the
school of oppression. We must therefore glance at the
previous history of the land of her birth.

The traveler, who at the present day visits the Netherlands, sees with astonishment what energy, economy,
and untiring perseverance have accomplished. Where
now are seen flourishing cities, waving fields of corn,
or herds of cattle grazing on the green pastures, the
sea once held dominion, and is now restrained from reas-
serting its rights only by the immense barriers which
the people have raised between themselves and their
enemy. The name Holland or Hollowland expresses
the nature of the country, as scooped out, lying lower
than the sea. In their contest with the Spaniards, the
people made their dykes and sluices means of defense,
and thus employed their old enemy as an ally against
the new.

At the earliest period to which we can go back by
the light of authentic history, the marshes and islands
at the mouths of the Rhine, Meuse, and Schelde were
occupied by barbarous tribes, of whom the Batavi
a brave and warlike people were the most prominent,
and they were never conquered by the Romans but
became their most efficient allies. In due time the
Roman sceptre was broken, and the hordes of barba-

rians from the north who sacked the imperial city also
overran all parts of the empire. The Saxons, Frisii,
Franks and others took the place of the Batavi who now
disappear from history.

In the latter part of the **seventh century**, **Christian-**
ity was introduced into West Friesland, now North Holland, by Willibrod a Northumbrian priest. He came
by invitation of Pepin who had conquered the Fries-
landers, and was now desirous of their conversion to
Christianity. He was chosen because of the similar-
ity of their language to that of old English. After him,
Boniface, who also was an English monk, and who
became the celebrated missionary bishop of Germany,
visited Friesland, accompanied by a large body of clergy.
After having baptized thousands of the people, and
founded many churches, he was cruelly murdered at
Dokkum. By the introduction of the Christian religion
the foundations of civilization and freedom were laid.

The Netherlands now came under the dominion of
the Franks. Charlemagne, who was crowned King of
the Franks in 768, and Emperor of the Romans in 800,
died at Aix-la-Chapelle in 814. The empire which he had
organized, and had governed with great energy, fell to
pieces after his death. Divided counsels and weakened
authority followed, and the various provinces of the
Netherlands, obliged to take care of themselves, were
governed by counts and dukes who paid homage to the
emperors.*

* "The counts at this time were officers appointed during
pleasure by the sovereigns to administer justice, and superintend military affairs in the cities and provinces, a certain
number of whom were placed under the authority of one duke.
Many of the dukes and counts rendered their power hereditary
and independent under the successors of Charlemagne in
France and Germany." Du Cange in Comites et Duces quoted
in Davies' History of Holland and the Dutch, vol. I, p. 19.

These counts and dukes were continually involved in wars, and the provinces were often torn by internal dissensions. In the fifteenth century the whole of the Netherlands came under the authority of one lord of the soil, Charles the Bold, Duke of Burgundy, whose daughter Maria married Maximilian of Austria. In this way, the Netherlands became a part of the hereditary possessions of the House of Austria. Their son, Philip the Fair, married Joanna, daughter of Ferdinand and Isabella of Spain, and the fruit of their union was the celebrated Charles V, hereditary monarch of Spain, Austria, the Sicilies, the Spanish possessions in America, and the Netherlands. Thus, the Netherlands came under the yoke of Spain, a subjection fraught with woes to which the history of the world scarcely presents a parallel. Charles ascended the throne of Spain in 1516, one year before the appearance of Luther as a reformer, and he was elected Emperor of Germany in 1519.

There is very much in the history of the Netherlands previous to the Reformation to awaken interest and excite admiration. The prosperity of the Southern Netherlands during the fourteenth and fifteenth centuries was remarkable. As we now walk through the quiet streets of those quaint old towns, Bruges, Ghent, and Antwerp, we find it hard to realize that at one time they were the marts for the commerce of the world, that traders from all countries thronged their fairs, that their streets were crowded with the thrifty sons of toil, by whom the most beautiful and costly fabrics were wrought, and that their merchants lived in princely luxury which was a marvel to the rest of Europe.

In these free towns the spirit of liberty was nourished, the people became jealous of their rights, and often broke out in bold resistance. Ghent was regarded as the hot-bed of sedition, and the burghers of Bruges

at one time restrained Maximilian himself of his liberty, until he had made concessions demanded by
them.

During this period the people also made progress in
the arts. The Dutch and Flemish painters became celebrated. It is claimed that the art of printing was in-
vented by Lawrence Koster, of Harlem, in 1423. Classical studies were pursued with great zeal and success
among them, and an immense impulse was given to
their commerce by the discovery of America in 1492,
and also of a new route to the East Indies by doubling
the Cape of Good Hope.

Like the rest of Europe this country was lying in the
darkness and under the curse of Popery. God's word
was hidden, the traditions of men were followed, the
cardinal doctrines of the Gospel were obscured, and
religion thought to consist in the worship of saints,
adoration of relics, and observance of ceremonies; and
whenever a faint ray of light appeared it was speedily
quenched.

But in due time light came that could not be quenched.
The lamp that was lighted at Glarus and Wittemberg
was brought into the Netherlands. The writings of
Zwingli, Luther and the other reformers were carried
every where with inconceivable rapidity, and the people eagerly received the words of life. But as England
had her Wyckliffe, and Bohemia her Huss and Jerome,
"morning stars" that shone before the rising of the
sun of the Reformation, so had Holland her Wessel
Gansevoort and Rudolf Agricola, natives of Groningen
and eminent scholars, who in the latter part of the fifteenth century, fifty years before Luther, studied the
Scriptures and came to the knowledge of the doctrine
of justification by faith, as well as the other cardinal
doctrines of the gospel.

Gansevoort or Wesselius, as he was frequently called, was celebrated for his attainments in theology. He taught at Heidelberg, Louvain, Paris, Rome, and finally settled in his native city of Groningen, in the neighborhood of which was a celebrated school over which he exerted great influence until his death in 1489. His views of evangelical truth were clear, and he denied many of the doctrines of the papacy, such as the authority of tradition, justification by works, the sacrifice of the mass, priestly absolution, purgatory, and papal infallibility. Luther became acquainted with the writings of Wesselius long after he himself had reached the gospel foundation, but so clearly did these writings contain his own evangelical views, that in order to prevent his enemies from using this fact to his disadvantage, he felt called upon solemnly to declare that he had not until then had knowledge of them, and that he was comforted and delighted with the confirmation of his faith afforded by them.

Agricola was distinguished for his attainments in Greek and Latin literature and in various sciences. He spent a great part of his life as a Professor at Heidelberg, and preceded Erasmus in applying the knowledge of Greek to the critical examination of the New Testament. In theological views he was in harmony with his friend and countryman Wesselius. The seed sown by these men was quickened into life by the Reformation.*

Erasmus, the eminent scholar of Rotterdam, by his bold exposures of the corruptions of the Church and the vices of the clergy, contributed not a little to convince the people of the need of a reformation. He at first encouraged the work, but when he saw that days

*Ullman's Reformers before the Reformation.

of danger were approaching, his faith and courage failed him. " Erasmus would have purified and repaired the venerable fabric of the Church with a light and cautious touch. fearful lest learning, virtue, and religion should be buried in its fall; while Luther struck at the tottering ruin with a bold and reckless hand, confident that a new and more beautiful temple would rise from its ashes." *

The gospel was extensively received. the Bible was accepted by very many as the only rule of faith, and the spread of evangelical doctrine was astonishingly rapid. But now began a mighty and protracted contest for freedom of conscience. A people who had been long accustomed to watch and fight for their civil rights might well be expected to contend for religious liberty. There was a call to it, for popery was ready to meet them with her favorite argument of persecution.

Charles, though not of a cruel temper, was devoted to the papal see, and was ready to use his power for the maintenance of its dominion over the minds and consciences of his subjects. Thinking himself called to root out the growing heresy, he did in his hereditary dominions of the Netherlands where he was free to act, what he could not do in Germany where he was trammeled by the Protestant princes. With promptness worthy of a better cause, he began as early as 1521, to issue the most severe edicts against his Protestant subjects in the Netherlands.

" By these, the reading of the Evangelists and Apostles, all open or secret meetings to which religion gave its name in ever so slight a degree, all conversations on the subject at home or at the table were forbidden

*Davies, Holland and the Dutch, Vol. I., p. 355.

under severe penalties. In every province special courts of judicature were established to watch over the execution of the edicts. Whoever held these erroneous opinions was to forfeit his office without regard to his rank. Whoever should be convicted of diffusing heretical doctrines, or even of simply attending the secret meetings of the Reformers, was to be condemned to death; and if a male, to be executed by the sword; if a female, to be buried alive. Backsliding heretics were to be committed to the flames. Not even the recantation of the offender could annul these appalling sentences. Whoever abjured his errors gained nothing by his apostasy but at furthest a milder kind of death." *

These edicts were unrelentingly executed during the reign of Charles by inquisitors appointed for the purpose, and tens of thousands suffered death, although these ministers of cruelty were greatly impeded in their work by the political institutions of the country and the independent spirit of the people.

Notwithstanding these cruelties, Charles was always popular in the Netherlands. He was a native of the country, spoke the language of the people, preferred their free manners to the reserve of the Spaniards, conferred office on natives, and was courteous in his intercourse with his subjects. "While his armies trod down their corn fields, while his rapacious imposts diminished their property, while his governors oppressed, his executioners slaughtered, he secured their hearts by a friendly demeanor."†

In the year 1555 occurred one of the most remarkable events of modern history, the voluntary abdication of Charles V. Enfeebled by disease, tired of the cares

*Schiller's Revolt of the Netherlands, p. 44.

†Schiller's Revolt, p. 46.

of Empire, and sick of its hollow splendors, a disappointed and dejected man, he resigned his crown, and retired to the monastery of Yuste in Spain to spend the remainder of his days in seclusion from the world. What a commentary on earthly glory! He had sown the wind and reaped the whirlwind. Never did a prince abuse such splendid opportunities for doing good to his subjects and to the world. How different would have been the course of events if Charles had favored or even tolerated the Reformation.

In a solemn convention at Brussels, Charles placed the sovereignty of the Netherlands in the hands of his son Philip, with the earnest desire and fond hope that the affection of the people for the father might be transferred to the son. Philip on his part took a solemn oath to respect the constitution of the states, the liberties, customs and usages of the people.*

In the character of Philip we find scarcely a single pleasing feature. He was a proud, gloomy bigot, reserved, cruel, revengeful. A Spaniard by birth, and educated by Spanish priests, he had nothing of the special attachment of his father to the people or country of the Netherlands. He had large ideas of authority, little generosity and no sympathy with the common people. Much as the states had suffered under Charles, they looked with dread to the assumption of power by his successor; for in his dark and gloomy visage they read at once of designs against their liberties, and they read correctly.† So far from profiting by the failure of his father's measures of persecution, he resolved to adopt them, and to prosecute them more vigorously, like the foolish Rehoboam who said to the people on his acces-

*Prescott's Philip II. Vol. I., p. 12.
†Schiller, p. 47.

sion to the throne, " My father made your yoke heavy, and I will add to your yoke ; my father also chastised you with whips, but I will chastise you with scorpions." *

It was his settled determination at all hazards to root out the Protestant faith from his dominions, being, as he said, more willing to be without subjects than to be a king of heretics. He violated his oath, broke every pledge, and continually planned new measures of greater severity.

Philip left the Netherlands in 1559 and committed the government to his sister Margaret, Duchess of Parma. He was anxious to introduce the Spanish Inquisition, but knowing that such a measure would produce an immediate and universal rebellion, he satisfied himself with obtaining a remodeling of the Church, by forming thirteen new bishoprics, which were under his control, and which he filled with men who were ready to do his pleasure.

It was claimed that the interests of the Church required this measure, for hitherto there had been only four bishoprics in the whole country. But the people understood the intent of this measure, and they saw in it a serious encroachment on their liberties ; for all these new ecclesiastics, were to be clothed with inquisitorial powers, and to be entitled to seats in the Assemblies of the States, where they would act of course, not : friends of the people, but as servants of the king. Chief among these was Cardinal Granvelle, a man of extraordinary abilities and unbounded and unscrupulous ambition, who was made archbishop of Mechlin, primate of the Netherlands and chief counselor of the regent.

*1. Kings. xii : 14.

The work of persecution now received a fresh
impulse; the officers of the dreaded tribunal were
everywhere at work, and tempting rewards were offered
for the betrayal and apprehension of the so-called heretics. Yet the gospel spread rapidly, there was an
enthusiasm for martyrdom, and many went to the stake
singing psalms of praise in which the multitude joined.

The various encroachments that were constantly made
upon the liberties of the country filled the minds of the
nobles, Catholic and Protestant alike, with serious
alarm. Some who were in the council of the regent
remonstrated, and letters and embassies were sent to
Philip, but all to no purpose. At last a large number,
chiefly of the lower nobility, bound themselves by a
solemn oath to protect one another against the Inquisition. A body of two hundred or more proceeded to
Brussels to present a petition to the regent, in which,
while they made the most emphatic professions of loyalty, they asked relief for their bleeding country by
the suppression of the Inquisition, and the repeal of all
oppressive edicts on the subject of religion. As they
came on foot with their petition, the Count of Barlai-
mont whispered in the ear of the regent, who seemed
somewhat disconcerted, that "they were nothing but a
crowd of beggars." This title, applied to them in deri-
sion, they adopted and proclaimed themselves the "Confederacy of the Gueux." *

The formation of this league filled the regent with
alarm and greatly encouraged the holders of evangelical truth. They were emboldened to profess their opinions and to perform their worship more openly. In
some places the mob, urged by fanatical zeal, broke into
the churches and threw down pictures, images, and

*Davies,' vol. I., p. 522.—Gueux, French for beggar.—Pres-
cott's Philip II, Vol I]., p. 12.

altars. In Flanders alone, four hundred churches were despoiled in a fortnight. This resort to violence was unjustifiable, was by no means encouraged by the confederate nobles, nor by the leading advocates of the evangelical doctrines; but it afforded Philip a pretext for the introduction of new and still more severe measures.

Divided counsels, lack of means, and dissensions among the nobles artfully fomented by the government, interfered much with the efficiency of the league; and many of the Catholic members left it when they saw the excesses of the image breakers, and after a series of reverses in the civil war that ensued, it was broken up. But though temporary and unsuccessful, this league had a powerful influence on the affairs of the Netherlands. In 1572, when the Duke of Alva was in power, William van de Mark in command of a fleet of twenty-four vessels, being refused permission to enter the ports of Denmark or Sweden, turned to England as his only resource; but Elizabeth, menaced by Philip in case protection should be afforded to the Gueux, refused to harbor him and his fleet. Driven to desperation they sailed for the Texel, with the intent of attacking the Spanish ships of war lying there, but being forced by the weather to enter the Meuse, they took possession of the town of Bril at the mouth. This was the beginning of open hostilities and it encouraged resistance in various parts of the country.*

The evangelicals were meanwhile, fast tending to efficient Church organization. For many years, they were

---

*Davies,' Vol. I., p. 577.—Bril is the Dutch for spectacles. Hence the jeu-de-mot:

"De Eerste dach von April
Verloor Due d'Alva zynen Bril."

compelled to worship secretly, and they called themselves "Der Nederlandsche kercken die onder't Cruis
sitten."—The churches of the Netherlands which sit
under the Cross." The confession of faith composed
by Guido de Bres in 1559 was published in 1561, was
adopted by the Synod of Antwerp in 1566, and by that of
Wesel in 1568. It was modeled after the confession of
the Reformed Church of France, contained thirty-seven
articles, and is one of the standards of doctrine of the
Church in America at the present day.

Perhaps nothing tended more to the spread of the
Reformation than public field-preaching, which was
begun almost simultaneously in the southern and northern provinces; in the former by Herman Stryker to a
congregation of some thousands in a field near Ghent;
in the latter by Jan Arentsen near the City of Hoorn.
These examples were speedily followed in all parts of
the country and multitudes every where assembled to
listen to the popular stirring eloquence of the preachers. On these occasions infants were presented for
baptism, the marriage ceremony was performed, collections for the poor were made, and the Psalms, which
had just been translated into Low Dutch were sung with
enthusiasm by the vast congregations.*

Three pastors were about this time set over the
Church of Amsterdam, Jan Arentsen, Peter Gabriel
and Nicholas Scheltius, men of zeal, self-denial, simple
manners and greatly endeared to the flock. Deacons
and deaconesses were appointed at the same time to
administer alms without distinction of persons.† It
is probable that many churches were secretly formed

---

*Schiller, q. 174. Prescott, Vol. II., p. 22, Brandt's Ref.
ormation, Vol. I., p. 172.

† Le Long Reformatie en Amsterdam p. 531 ;

on the Genevan Presbyterian model, for in 1559 rewards were offered for the apprehension of a minister, elder, or deacon; and in 1568 the representatives of these churches met in Synod at Wesel on the Rhine because unable to do so safely in the Netherlands, and there they provisionally adopted rules of Church government and order.

The cup of misery for the Netherlands was not yet full. Philip exasperated by the conduct of the nobles, enraged by the obstinacy of the people, mortified by the failure of all his measures to extirpate heresy, and driven to desperation, forced the publication of the decrees of the Council of Trent, and determined that the extremest measures of persecution should be vigorously employed. He had hitherto feared to send a Spanish army; but it now came composed of 10,000 men headed by that monster of cruelty the Duke of Alva, who appeared to the terror of the country in 1567 and unfortunately, just at the time when through the decided measures of the regent, quiet seemed to have been restored. He immediately established a court of twelve members which he called the "Council of Tumults" from its professed design to bring to justice those who had created disturbances; but the people more appropriately called it the "Council of Blood." By this court of which the cruel Vargas was the leading member, the most horrible atrocities were committed. The Counts Egmond and Hoorn were entrapped, insulted with a mock trial, and beheaded in the market place at Brussels. Death was decreed against all who had signed the petition against the Inquisition, all who had been in any way connected with the image-breakers, all who had heard a sermon, sung a psalm, or given lodging to a heretical preacher. Every refinement of torture was used, and it was the boast of Alva that in the space of seven years, no less than eighteen thousand persons had perished by the hands of the executioner beside those who had fallen in battle. One hundred thousand houses were deserted, their inmates having fled for refuge to other nations. Very many of these refugees found their way to England and introduced into that country the useful manufactures in which they had been engaged in their own land.

This darkest hour of the night heralded the morning. William of Orange was God's chosen instrument for the deliverance of this oppressed people.

He was born at Dillenburg in Germany, was sent when eleven years of age to the court of Maria of Hungary, was taken into the confidence of Charles V., and when a mere youth was put in command of an army against France. On Philip's accession to the throne he stood at the head of the nobility of the Netherlands, and was made stadtholder of Holland, Zealand, and Utrecht, and also one of the counselors of the regent Margaret on the departure of Philip to Spain.* He remained in the council as long as he could,

---

*The Stadtholder was Captain-general and Admiral of the land and naval forces of the Republic. His dignity was originally not hereditary, but elective by the provinces. During war he disposed of all military grades, and conducted all military operations as General-in-chief. The Stadtholder being at the same time, Admiral of the naval forces of the Republic, the commanders of the separate fleets were called Lieutenant-admirals. The Stadtholder might at any time enter the hall of the States General and propose public measures, but he had no vote and no right to deliberate. During his presence debate was suspended ; and when the object of his visit was attained, he left the assembly. After William I, the dignity of Stadtholder was continued by successive elections in the family of the Prince of Orange until 1672, when William III. procured it to be made hereditary."—Brodhead's History of New York, Vol. I., p. 450.

speaking often boldly and faithfully against the oppressive measures that were pursued, until a little before the arrival of Alva he was compelled by the arbitrary demands of the regent to resign his position. He retired to his hereditary possessions in Germany, and with an anxious mind watched the progress of affairs in the Netherlands, while many exiles gathered around him and entreated him to interpose for the suffering country. At last he consented, enlisting his four brothers in the cause. At his and their own expense chiefly, an army was raised and the contest with Alva began. The northern provinces at once rallied around William who gained so many advantages that Alva resigned his office and left the country in 1573.

William was called "the silent," not on account of a taciturn disposition, but because when the king of France revealed to him that he had agreed with the king of Spain that all the Protestants in the country should be destroyed, he maintained silence, kept his own counsel, and formed his plans for service and sacrifice for his country. He was as able to read the thoughts and plans of others as he was to conceal his own. He has been accused of selfish and ambitious aims, but how can the genuineness of his patriotism be questioned if we judge him by his works and sacrifices? He was opposed to all violent, revolutionary measures, hoping through petition to obtain a just administration of affairs, and he resorted to arms only when nothing else remained to be done; but then he was ready to sacrifice his all. His uncommon sagacity, wisdom, caution, perserverance and steadfast devotion to the cause of civil liberty none can deny, nor question his rightful claim to the title given him by a grateful people of "Father of their Fatherland."

He was taught the Protestant faith in his childhood,

but when he became an attendant at courts, he was trained in and he conformed to the Romish or Court religion. On his retirement to Germany he made the subject of religion one of special study and returned to the faith of the Reformation.* Whether that faith was embraced with the understanding merely, or with the heart also, is known only to God, though we cannot but hope that divine grace had entered the heart of one who after the loss of three brothers could write to the sole remaining one as follows: "On account of my grief, I scarcely know what to do. Notwithstanding, we must always acquiesce in God's will, trusting in the Providence of Him who has given the blood of His own Son for the benefit of His Church, and believing that He will do nothing but what shall in the end be for His own glory, and the establishment of the Church. Although to the world it may seem impossible, and although we should all return, and the people all perish, yet we may be sure that God will always see to His own cause."†

Is it strange that a people who had such a leader manifested extraordinary courage and endurance? For examples of their spirit we need only refer to the sieges of Harlem, Alkmaar and Leyden, in defense of which cities the women and children stood side by side with the men. When the people of Leyden, mad with hunger, demanded of one of the burgomasters,‡ Peter Vanderwerf, that he should give them food or treat for the surrender of the city, he replied: "I have made an oath, which, by the help of God, I will keep, that

*M. Groen's "Kort Overzigt," p. 38.

†Prescott's Philip II., Vol. II., pp. 93, 127.

‡"To the burgomasters was committed the care of the police and the ammunition, of the public peace, and of cleansing and victualling the town."—Davies, Vol. I., p. 77.

your friend and servant
J. H. Livingston

I will never yield to the Spaniard. Bread, as you well know, I have none; but if my death can serve you, slay me, cut my body into morsels, and divide it amongst you." The burghers,* called to the enemy from the walls. "You found all your arguments on the misery and famine that threaten us; you say that we are eaters of dogs and cats: know that when this food shall fail us, we have each a left arm which we will eat while we preserve our right to drive the tyrant and his blood-thirsty bands from our walls; and if God shall, as we have justly merited, deliver us into your hands, we will ourselves set fire to our city rather than become your slaves."† The dykes were cut, and relief came over the waters to the starving people after they had endured the siege five months. The Prince of Orange wishing to reward them for their bravery, offered to give them an annual fair or a university as they might prefer, and they immediately chose the latter, and so the famous university of Leyden originated.

When the states took up arms against Alva they had no idea of throwing off the yoke of Spain.‡ In a petition to the king they said: "Since they, (the duke and his creatures) take pleasure in our death, and think it their

---

*" Burghership was generally obtained by the payment of a sum of money, and the registry of the citizen's name upon the roll of burghers. It was hereditary. It could pass by marriage, and it could be acquired by females as well as by males. Foreigners also, after a year's probation could become burghers. The burgher-right gave to the citizen freedom of trade, exemption from tolls, special privileges and favors in prosecutions, and an exclusive eligibility to municipal office.—Brodhead's New York, Vol. I. p. 453.

†Davies, Vol. II., p. 12.

‡The legislative assembly of each province was called " the States" of that province. The States General was composed of deputies from the provinces.

interest to be our murderers, we will much rather die an honorable death for the liberties and welfare of our dear country than submit to be trampled under foot by insolent foreigners, who have always hated or envied us. By so doing we shall at least transmit to our posterity this fame and reputation, that their ancestors scorned to be slaves to a Spanish Inquisition, and therefore made no scruple of redeeming a scandalous life by an honorable death. We contend for nothing less than freedom of conscience, our wives and children, our lives and fortunes. We do not desire to be discharged from our allegiance to your Majesty, but only that our conscience may be preserved free before the Lord our God, that we may be permitted to hear His holy word, and walk in His commandments, so that we may be able to give an account of our souls to the Supreme Judge at the last day."*

But Providence led the people to freedom by a way that they had not devised. In 1572 an assembly of the states was held at Dordrecht by which William was proclaimed stadtholder of Holland, Zealand, Friesland and Utrecht. The states of Holland at the same time felt compelled for their own safety to expel the Romanists from the churches and to establish the Reformed religion. This measure was carried with some difficulty, but it was felt to be necessary inasmuch as the ecclesiastics were the sworn friends of Spain. They, however, did not, forgetting their own struggles for freedom of conscience, proceed to persecute the Romanists, but decreed that "not only all religions ought to be tolerated, but that all restraint in matters of religion was as detestable as the Inquisition itself.

*Magazine of the Ref. Dutch Church, Vol. I., p. 354.
*Brodhead, Vol. I., p. 100.

In the year 1579 the foundations of the Republic were fairly laid in the formation at Utrecht of the Union of the Seven Provinces. The motto, "Eendracht maakt macht" "Union makes strength," was adopted. The provinces were driven to this union and they found strength and glory in it; the rights of conscience were again confirmed by William; two years later (1581), allegiance to Spain was renounced, independence was formally declared, and Philip was deposed. To appreciate this bold and noble step we must bear in mind the notions of the day in regard to the divine right of kings, and we will see that the declaration of independence issued on this occasion, in its assertion of republican principles, was far in advance of the common sentiment of the age. The following extract will suggest that it was not unknown to the illustrious men who in 1776 drafted our own:

"The States-General of the United Provinces of the Netherlands to all who shall see or read these presents, greeting: Whereas, It is notorious to every one that the prince of a country is established by God as a sovereign chief of his subjects to defend and preserve them from all injuries, oppressions, and violences, as a shepherd is ordained for the defense and protection of his flock; and that subjects are not created of God for the sake of the prince, to be obedient to him in all that he commands, whether it be pious or impious, just or unjust, and to serve him as his slaves; but that the prince is made for the subjects, without whom he cannot be prince, in order to govern them according to right and reason, and maintain and love them as a father his children, or a shepherd his flock, who risks his person and life to defend and protect them. And when he does not do this, but instead of defending his subjects, seeks to oppress them and to deprive them of their privileges and ancient customs, and commands them and uses them as slaves, he ought not to be deemed a prince but a tyrant; and as such, his subjects, according to right and reason, can no longer recognize him as their prince, especially when this is done with deliberation and by the authority of the States of the country, but they can abandon him, and without any impropriety choose another in his place as chief and lord to defend them."

The declaration then recites the conditions on which the Dutch had remained in allegiance, and the grievances they had suffered from the Spanish government, and then concludes as follows:

"We therefore, make it known that from the foregoing considerations and pressed by extreme necessity as we have said, we have with one accord, deliberation, and consent, declared, and do declare, the king of Spain deposed ipso jure from his sovereignty, right and heritage in these countries, and that we have no longer any intention of recognizing him in anything touching the prince, or his sovereignty, jurisdiction, or domains in these Lower Countries, and that we shall no longer use his name as sovereign, nor shall we permit any one thus to make use of it, for we have found this to be expedient for the good of the country. And to do this, and all that may result, we give to all those whom it may concern, full power, authority and special command. In witness whereof we have hereto set our seal. Given at the Hague, in our assembly, July 26th 1581.*

What review of the object and powers of government could be more clear and just than that which the States of the Netherlands set forth in this document more than three hundred years ago? What improvement has been made on it in this day of boasted progress of

*Brodhead, Vol. I., Appendix p. 760.

liberal principles? The adoption of such a paper well entitles Holland to the name that has been given her, "Mother of Free States."

The Dutch republic increased in strength and prosperity from day to day. The Reformation having been crushed in southern Netherlands, many lovers of the evangelical doctrines came to the northern provinces to find an asylum, and many also came from Germany, and many Huguenots from France. This little country rose rapidly to importance as a commercial nation, and in a few years became mistress of the seas. Even while fighting for her rights, she was extending her trade to every land, and her merchantmen came home laden with riches from the ends of the earth. The arts and sciences and literature were cultivated with zeal and success, and in every department of learning, divinity, law, politics, medicine, the fine arts, and military and naval science, the sons of Holland stood in the seventeenth century, in the front rank. In divinity the renowned names of Junius, Gomarus, Arminius, Cocceius, and Voetius represent a host. In political science who of their age excelled Olden Barneveldt and the De Witts? In naval affairs, what names occur more readily to the reader of history than Heemskerk, Tromp and De Ruyter? Of classical scholars we need only mention Scaliger and Heinsius; of philosophers, Grotius, Plancius and Spinoza; of physicians, Boerhaave and Tulp; of historians, Brandt, De Laet and Van Meteren; of artists, Gerard Douw, Rembrandt, Vandervelde and Wouvermans; of poets, Cats and Vondel, the former "remarkable for purity of diction, felicity of description and tenderness of sentiment; the latter "distinguished for the lofty fire of his imagination, the grandeur of his conceptions, and the vigor of his expression."*

*Davies, Vol. II., p. 667.

The rights of conscience were sacredly guarded by the Republic. The Reformed faith of the Calvinistic type was the established national religion; but by its side every form of doctrine and worship was freely tolerated, and the Romanist and Lutheran were each permitted in his own way to worship God. The Jew, hunted as an outlaw in every other country, was here welcomed, and Holland became the place of refuge for all who in any part of Europe were oppressed on account of their religion. Walloon churches were established by refugees from Belgium and France using the French language; Scotch churches by the Presbyterians from Scotland; the Pilgrims of England dwelt at Leyden twelve years before they embarked for America; and the Non-conformists of England found, on the restoration of the Stuarts a resting place in Holland. These last simply exchanged places with Charles who returned from exile to drive them into it. Amsterdam was reproached as a "common harbor of all opinions and of all heresies." Andrew Marvell wrote in not very friendly rhyme,

> " Hence Amsterdam, Turk, Christian, Pagan, Jew,
>   Staple of sects, and mint of schism grew.
>   That bank of conscience, where not one so strange
>   Opinion, but finds credit and exchange:
>   In vain for Catholics ourselves we bear,
>   The universal church is only there."

It was a day of great mourning through the land, when William of Orange was removed from the head of the Republic by his assassination at Delft in 1584. As he fell, he exclaimed, "My God, my God, have mercy on my soul, and on this unhappy people." The Stadtholdership was conferred upon his son Maurice, a youth of seventeen years, but a son worthy of his sire. The people were at first greatly disheartened, and the Spaniards improved the opportunity to attempt the recovery of much that had been lost. But soon, aid came from England to the great joy of the people, the Earl of Leicester being sent by Queen Elizabeth with a body of troops. In the view of the Pope, this was a heinous crime on the part of Elizabeth, and he in the exercise of his blasphemously assumed function of Prince of the Kings of the earth, at once proceeded to depose her. The execution of the sentence devolved on Philip, who as his obedient subject, prepared and sent to sea, what he proudly called the "Invincible Armada," which was scattered and destroyed in sight of the shores of England.

Maurice was an able statesman and successful general, and after a series of victories over the Spaniards, a truce for twelve years was agreed upon with Spain. This period of rest was well improved by the Netherlands, by the increase of her commerce and resources, and the strengthening of her institutions. It was, however, marked by fearful internal troubles, by contentions in Church and State and by the disputes between the Gomarists and Arminians which resulted in the calling of the Synod of Dort, and the condemnation of the Arminian doctrines.

At the end of the truce hostilities were resumed, but Spain was no longer formidable. Maurice died in 1625, and his brother Frederic Henry was elected Stadtholder of most of the Provinces, and under his wise and excellent government great prosperity was enjoyed. Meanwhile Philip II. and also Philip III. passed from the scene, and in 1648 the independence of the United Provinces was formally acknowledged by Philip IV. Thus ended a contest which had been carried on for nearly three generations by three successive tyrants of Spain, resisted by three successive Princes of the House of Orange.

The reader will mark in this wonderful history the hand of God, who defeateth the counsel of princes and scattereth their armies. We stand in awe as we contemplate how the pride of Spain, the proudest and at that time most powerful kingdom in Europe was humbled by a people inhabiting reclaimed marshes occupying a country so destitute of natural resources that bread for their support, and the stones and timber for the dykes needed for their protection had to be brought from other lands. For eighty years this memorable struggle of weakness with power was continued with untiring perseverance, and the people not only succeeded in the end, but they grew during the strife, and gathered strength while walking in the fires, so that long before their independence was acknowledged, they commanded the admiration of the world for their progress in art, science, and literature, for the extent of their commerce, for the strength of their government, and for their power by sea and land. It was the Lord's doing and it is marvelous in our eyes.

But inasmuch as God works by agencies, it is exceedingly interesting as well as profitable to trace them. In this instance very many contributed to bring about the result. Philip strangely mistook the character of the people, and adopted the very policy that was sure to defeat his purpose. Persuaded that the suppression of heresy would be the work of a day only, and that his father had failed through excess of leniency, he adopted severer measures; but this very course instead of subduing the so-called heretics, roused the Catholics to become their allies.

Many of the causes of the success of the Dutch are fully traced in Davies' History of Holland, to which the reader is referred, as we can only glance at them.* Much

*Vol. II, p. 653.

is to be attributed to the moral qualities of the people.
Their known integrity commanded universal confidence,
and placed at their disposal the treasuries of other
nations. The advantage of this appeared in the promptness and vigor of their action, and in the contentment
and spirit of their well-paid soldiery.

They were remarkably firm and persevering. Their
patient struggle with the ocean for ground to stand
upon, trained them for endurance in the contest for
rights without which the soil would have been of little
value. They looked with singleness of eye to the work
before them, and would not be diverted by side issues,
nor drawn off by flattering temptations, nor driven
from it by threats of imprisonment, banishment or
death. "The goal which they had determined to reach
did not change its position from day to day as whim,
ambition or circumstances dictated. In their deepest
reverses, at their highest elevation of prosperity, it was
still the same. They pursued their path toward it with
slow and measured steps, and when at last they attained
it, they suffered no disappointment, they experienced
no reaction. They did not, as it too often happens, in the
bitterness of deceived hope, rush back to a condition
worse than that they had left, but were content to find
what they had sought, freedom and security; and riches,
glory and honor were added to them."

They were quiet, unselfish patriots, seemingly careless of personal glory, but wrapped up in the cause of the
country. Spanish gold, though freely offered could not
bribe one of them; the country was everything, the
individual nothing.

Their household economy enabled them to pour mil-
lions into the exhausted national treasury when they
were needed. The highest officers of the government,
and the military and naval commanders lived in the

most modest and frugal style. And every housewife carefully husbanded resources for the help of the struggling country.

The nation abounded in men of marked ability, for the discipline to which it was subjected, could not fail to train and strengthen the intellect. Her statesmen and diplomatists took their stand by the side of the leading minds of the French, Spanish and English governments.

Much was due to the navy, which very early became the right arm of defence; the naval commanders of the republic covered themselves with unfading glory.

The prevalent form of municipal government was of no little advantage. Every town in the confederacy was in a sense independent, and hence a serious blow in one quarter did not result in the destruction of the whole. Besides, the rights which the towns had gained, little by little, from the earliest periods, were well known to the people who were accustomed to discuss and jealously to guard them.

The geographical position and physical features of the country were favorable. Their harbors while dangerous to an ignorant enemy, were places of security for their own ships brought in by their experienced pilots. The northern part of the country could be traversed by an army only in the winter, while all along the coast, the sea was in waiting, a ready ally more powerful than troops. Holland was also greatly strengthened by the influx of multitudes of the best people from southern Netherlands, France, Germany and England, who here found refuge from persecution and who identified themselves with their protectors and strengthened their hands.

It is impossible to estimate how much the world owes to this protracted but successful contest in the Nether-

lands. The opposition of Philip was to Protestantism
or what he called heresy, and to liberty not only in the
Netherlands, but in England, France, everywhere. How
much America owes to the firm maintenance of the
rights of conscience there, who can tell? The Pilgrim
Fathers have been covered with glory by their descendants and justly; but, surely justice can be done to others
without treason to them. It will not be denied that
to Holland belongs the glory of having been the first
of modern nations to guarantee liberty of conscience
in matters of religion. This liberty has always been
claimed by oppressed individuals, and contended for by
oppressed bodies of men, but where was the government or party in power that was willing to concede it?
Nay, the weak who had fought for the rights of conscience, and secured them for themselves, were ready
to deny them to others, and the oppressed became the
oppressors. In England, the Roman Catholic and Protestant by turns persecuted and were persecuted. In
the new world to which the Puritan had come to enjoy
liberty of conscience, he denied it to the Baptist and
Quaker; and sorry we are to admit that one governor
of New Netherland, on his own responsibility annoyed
the Lutheran, Independent and Quaker, for which he
was promptly rebuked by the proper authorities. Nay,
Holland was once derelict to her own principles, though
under palliating circumstances when she banished the
Arminian preachers. That exception has attracted
particular notice from the very fact that there was a
constitutional guarantee of the rights of conscience;
and surely the dwelling together of Romanist and Jew,
Lutheran and Calvinist, each worshiping in his own
way was proof that it was by no means a dead letter.

At Leyden, the Hollanders and the Pilgrim Fathers
dwelt together in Christian fellowship, and the twelve

years spent there by the latter were not spent in vain 'while in contact with the institutions of this free and powerful republic. The Pilgrims came from their place of refuge and planted their colony at Plymouth, while the Dutch brought their institutions to New Netherland. Let us gratefully acknowledge the agency of each in laying the foundation for civil liberty, good government, freedom in religious and educational institutions in this land, and let us sturdily deny a monopoly of praise to either. All of good that we possess did not come out of the cabin of the Mayflower, but Providence has gathered choice materials out of the various nations of Europe, and brought them to these western shores for the erection of a temple to His praise.

CHAPTER II.

SETTLEMENT OF DOCTRINE, POLITY AND WORSHIP.

In the early part of the seventeenth century the United Provinces rose to a new and glorious position before the nations of Europe. These had with various interest watched their protracted contest with Spain, expecting to witness the end of it in their ruin. But now the pride of Spain was humbled, and in the year 1609, a truce, or cessation of hostilities for twelve years, was agreed upon under conditions very favorable to the Dutch. From this time alliances with the Provinces were courted by powers of the first rank. By means of the East India Company, a most extensive and lucrative trade was carried on with the East, and the supremacy of the Dutch was established in the Asiatic seas.

The enemies of the Dutch Republic had predicted that just as soon as contention with the enemy should cease, domestic dissensions would arise, and these malicious predictions were sadly fulfilled, for serious divisions quickly arose in both church and state. The brilliant military career of Maurice had brought him unbounded influence with the army and the people. Being now stadtholder of five provinces, he was in a very favorable position to prosecute any ambitious designs that he might entertain. John von Olden Barneveldt, the celebrated advocate of the Province of Holland, looked with a jealous eye on Maurice, suspected him of an intention to overthrow the constitution and to grasp after absolute power. He devoted himself to the work of watching and curbing the prince, and of guarding the authority and prerogatives of the States General.

Barneveldt was a man of extraordinary ability, and an accomplished statesman, who for a long time had the management of foreign affairs, and in that department had rendered his country signal service. By his skillful diplomacy the cautionary towns which England had long held as security for moneys loaned, were redeemed on liberal terms. Maurice became exceedingly impatient of the vast influence of the advocate who seemed to be in his way, and there arose "a mutual antipathy which soon deepened on the side of the stadtholder into a sentiment of intense animosity against Barneveldt, and which the sacrifice of its hated object at length could scarcely appease." * The execution of Barneveldt was a sad ending to what seems to have been chiefly an intensely bitter, personal controversy between two ambitious high dignitaries. We cannot doubt that Maurice, who fought so heroically for his country, was a true patriot, and Barneveldt as well, who labored so zealously and sucessfully for it in the sphere of diplomacy.

Closely interwoven with the political difficulties of this period was an ecclesiastical one, called the Arminian controversy. The weaker and subdued party usually receives the sympathy of posterity, and so, most writers on this subject have been far from concealing their opinion that the Remonstrants or Arminians were hardly dealt with, and were persecuted throughout. The candid reader of the history will undoubtedly discover faults in temper and measure on both sides, and will probably be inclined to make a pretty equal distribution of them. This, however, does not affect the questions of truth in regard to the controverted points,

*Brodhead, Vol. I., p. 108.

nor of fact, nor of the reasonableness of a call for a national synod which was demanded by the opponents of the doctrines of Arminius.*

The ground of this controversy should be clearly understood. It has been said that from the beginning of the Reformation to the Synod of Dort, there was no uniformity of doctrine required of the ministers and churches in the Netherlands, but that during this period young preachers came from the school of Calvin and Beza into the country, who taught the peculiar doctrines of that school, and endeavored to impose them on their brethren who for the most part, held the more moderate sentiments of Zwingli or Melancthon.†

This is a very unfair statement, for the opinions of Calvin and Beza were never referred to in the controversy. The fact is, that the Reformed Church of the Netherlands, though Calvinistic in doctrine, yet never acknowledged Calvin as master, but always appealed to the word of God. The charge against Arminius and his followers was, not that they taught doctrines opposed to those of Calvin but to those of the word of God, as exhibited in the Confession of Faith and Heidelberg Catechism which were acknowledged standards in the Church. It is true that at the first, and during the years before the churches could worship publicly, and synods be convened, there was no confession adopted by ecclesiastical authority and subscription to which was required. But even then, there was a substantial agreement in doctrine; and soon after the appearance of

* History of Events preceding the Call of the Synod of Dort published by authority of the States General and translated by the Rev. Thomas Scott, D.D., Acta Synodi Dordracensis. Brandt's Reformation in the Low Countries. Vanderkemp's Schets Dordsche Synode.

† Calder's Memoirs of Episcopius, p. 23.

the Belgic Confession and Heidelberg Catechism, these were adopted by the first Synods, and assent to them was demanded of all the ministers as early as 1571. The charge against Arminius was that he taught doctrines contrary to the standards to which, as a minister, he had subscribed.

In the year 1602 one of the professorships of theology in the University of Leyden was made vacant by the death of Junius. Jacobus (Harmensen) Arminius was at the time pastor in Amsterdam, where his orthedoxy had been called in question by the consistory, who had stayed further proceedings on his declaration that he agreed with the confession and catechism, and that he received the doctrines contained in them as they were commonly understood by the Church. This consistory as well as the deputies of the Synod opposed his appointment to the vacant chair at Leyden. But at a conference held with Gomarus, one of the professors, and in presence of the deputies of the Synod and also of the curators of the University. he renewed his profession of adherence to the standards, and promised that he would teach nothing at variance with the received doctrines of the Church. His nomination was thereupon confirmed, and he was inducted into his office by Gomarus himself.

For some time he refrained from publicly advancing anything contrary to these doctrines, but in a year or two he began craftily to instill into the minds of his pupils, the sentiments that had caused dissatisfaction at Amsterdam, and he was afterwards emboldened to proclaim them more openly though in ambiguous language. This led Gomarus to make a public and clear explanation of the received doctrine. The consistory of Leyden and the Synodal deputies, at once saw that there was a marked difference between the views of the

two professors, and they invited Arminius to a friendly
conference. This he declined, but he renewed the professions previously made, which were again accepted
and time was allowed him to prove his sincerity.

But the controversy, so far from being stayed, became
an open one spreading from the students to the
ministers and so to the people. The Classis of Dordrecht believing that measures should at once be taken
for its settlement, brought the matter before the Synod
of South Holland, which resolved to enquire into it;
but its deputies were put off by the curators of the
University with the plea that a National Synod would
soon be called to decide on the theological questions
involved. A petition for such a Synod was presented
to the States-General, who replied that authority had
already been granted for the calling of a synod, which
was indeed true, but connected with it was the condition
that the confession of faith and catechism should be
revised by the Synod, and to it the churches could not
give assent. This condition had been craftily introduced by the States of Holland, and so the calling of a
Synod was defeated from year to year. The States of
Holland had for a long time labored to destroy the
independence of the Church, and to make it completely
subservient to State policy, and they seized the opportunity to use these doctrinal difficulties for the attain-
ment of the desired end. The States sided with the
party which they believed would increase their own
power and diminish that of the Church. Hence the
proposal of the unacceptable condition on which alone
they would consent to authorize a call for a National
Synod; hence the order in 1608 that preachers should
make their sentiments in regard to the standards known,
not to the classes but to the Supreme Court of the
States; hence the suspension of the annual Synod;

hence the favorable reception of the remonstrance presented by the Arminian party; hence the order to the classes not to examine ministers and candidates on the disputed points, but to tolerate both views; hence the various measures infringing on the rights of the Church, ending with the prescription of an ambiguous and objectionable formulary of faith to be a rule for the guidance of consistories and classes under pain of severe penalties.*

The beginning of open, direct antagonism of the State to the Church was seen in bold interference with her discipline. The synods and classes deeming that the times demanded that all the ministers should be required to subscribe to the confession and catechism, which had in some cases been neglected, passed resolutions to that effect. Five of the ministers of the Classis of Alkmaar, with Venator, a man unsound in doctrine and immoral in life, as their leader, refused to do this, and they were consequently suspended from office. They appealed for redress to the States of Holland, and so the first resort to the civil authorities in matters of church discipline was made by the Arminian party. This started a controversy about the authority of the State in ecclesiastical matters, not unlike that, which, in later times resulted in Scotland in the coming out of the Free Church from the Establishment. The States flattered by this acknowledgment of their authority, and feeling that its exercise would go far to confirm and perpetuate it, ordered the classis to restore the suspended ministers. The classis declined to do this, on the ground that the States had no right to interfere in a matter of discipline that was purely ecclesiastical, and in this refusal the classis was sustained by the Synod of North Holland.

*Vanderkemp's "Schets Dordsche Synode," p. 17.

The death of Arminius, which occurred in 1609, did not put an end to the controversy, but on the contrary, it was maintained with much bitterness. His followers adopted a remonstrance which was sent to the States, from which they received the name of Remonstrants, whereby they are known in history. In this document they gave their views on the disputed points; they complained of the treatment they had received in their classes; and they asked for the protection of their persons and opinions against all church censures. They exhibited their sentiments under the five heads of—1, Predestination; 2, Redemption by the death of Christ; 3, Man's corruption; 4, God's grace in conversion; 5, Perseverance of the saints. They contended that their variations from the received doctrines, if any, were insignificant, though to others they seemed to be great. The opposite party replied to this remonstrance in a paper, from which they were called Contra-remonstrants.

The Curators of the University nominated as the successor of Arminius, Conradus Vorstius who was more than suspected of Socinianism, and this nomination was favored by the Remonstrants, who declared that they found nothing objectionable in his writings. This led their opponents to fear that they were ready to go further than they had professed, and that they would not hesitate even to break up the foundations of the faith; an opinion in which they were confirmed by noticing the intimacy of some of them with men of loose principles. Great excitement was created by the nomination of Vorstius, and even James of England protested against his appointment. His name was dropped, and Simon Episcopius was appointed to the professorship.

Separations and disturbances now began to take place in various parts of the country. At Rotterdam,

Geselius one of the Contra-remonstrant ministers was expelled from the city by the magistracy. Thus the Remonstrants were the first to use the "coercive force of the civil power, of which they afterward so bitterly complained, when turned against themselves."* That "coercive force" was employed in almost every town and riots broke out in many places. This led the States of Holland to pass what was called the "Severe Edict," in which they proclaimed their disapproval of a National Synod, and authorized the levy of Waardgelders or militia for the defence of the towns, a measure that served only to increase the unhappy disturbances.

Maurice at last felt himself called upon to interpose to the extent of his lawful authority. He has been reproached for placing himself at the head of one of the parties, and of using arbitrary and unauthorized measures against the other. Nothing can be more evident however than that down to 1617, he did not appear prominently in the controversy, and that the first measures he employed were of the mildest character. In that year a part of the congregation at the Hague with Roseus, one of the pastors, separated from the Remonstrant pastor, the distinguished Uytenbogard, and established worship by themselves. Maurice was now called upon by Barneveldt himself to interpose, which was an evident acknowledgment of his right and duty to do so. He was even rebuked by him for the lack of zeal he had hitherto manifested—a decisive refutation of the charge that he was a warm partisan through the whole controversy. Maurice thereupon referred to his oath, in which he had sworn to protect the Reformed Religion and declared that he would protect it; that a National Synod ought to be called; and that the Contra-remon-

*Davies, Vol. II., p. 465.

strants ought to be allowed to worship separately without losing their rights and privileges as members of the National Church. He himself worshiped with the Separatists at the Hague, and urged the States to grant the petition for the calling of a synod without delay. In the towns also where high-handed and lawless measures had been pursued, he used his authority to secure changes in the municipal governments. That this authority was to some extent arbitrarily exercised may well be believed, without admitting the truth of the wholesale charges that, to obtain his own ends, he trampled the rights of these towns under foot.*

Without entering into the details of the history or giving an opinion on the points in controversy, we recall attention to the relative positions of the two parties. The Contra-Remonstrants urged the calling of a National Synod as the only body that could lawfully decide whether the new teachings were in accordance with the doctrinal standards of the established Church. The Remonstrants on the other hand dreaded nothing more than the calling of such a synod, and as they were favored by the civil authorities, it was postponed from year to year. The Remonstrants insisted that in the call for the meeting of the Synod, a revision of the standards should be mentioned as a prominent object of such meeting. The Contra-remonstrants claimed that they were not opposed to such revision, but that they deemed it for manifest reasons unwise to put it into the call for the meeting of the Synod. The Remonstrants labored to create the impression that the points in dispute were not important, but that both views might be taught in the Church with mutual toleration, while the Contra-remonstrants contended that vital doctrines were

*Vanderkemp, p. 26.

assailed. When the Remonstrants found that the call
for a synod could no longer be delayed, they proposed
that, in order to secure an impartial judgment, its members should be appointed by the States-General, and
not by the Church in her regular way, according to her
government and discipline. This, of course, could not
be allowed. They also talked continually of pacific
measures; "measures which," one has well remarked,
"the weaker party always so strongly insists on,
and which they are so seldom found to practice,
when by a change of circumstances, they become the
stronger." *

A synod was at length called by the authority of the
States-General, and met at Dordrecht on the 13th of
November 1618 and its sessions extended over a period
of more than six months. From the churches of the
United Provinces thirty five ministers and twenty
elders were present as delegates and also five Professors of Theology, from the five schools of Leyden, Frane-
ker, Groningen, Harderwyck and Middleburg. There
were also twenty-seven delegates present from the
churches of Great Britain, the Palatinate, Hesse, Swit-
zeland, Geneva, Bremen, East Friesland and Nassau.
The delegates from the French churches were forbidden by their king to attend. Eighteen political commissioners, deputed by the States-General, were present to watch the proceedings. The learning and integrity of the members of this synod cannot be questioned.
Among them we find the names of Polyander, Lubberti,
Waleus, Faukelius, Damman, Hommius, Trigland,
Voetius, and Scultetus. At the head of the English dep-
utation was George Carleton, Bishop of Llandaff, and
connected with him were Joseph Hall, Dean of

*Davies, Vol. II., p. 483.

Worcester, Samuel Ward, Archdeacon of Taunton, John Davenant, Professor of theology at Cambridge, and Walter Balcancall representing the Church of Scotland.

Rev. Johannes Bogerman, pastor of the church of Leeuwarden was chosen President. The proceedings were conducted in Latin, and the members were sworn to refer all disputed questions to the word of God for decision. Thirteen of the Remonstrant ministers were cited to appear, who immediately, through their spokesman, Episcopius, attempted to justify themselves and endeavored to turn the Synod from an ecclesiastical court into a conference for the interchange of opinions, denying also that its members were lawful and impartial judges. The Synod on the other hand considered itself to be a court acting judicially in the trial of accused persons. The cited persons presented a written statement of their views, but declined to give such oral explanations as were asked. The Synod, wearied at last, by what they regarded as pertinacious evasions, summarily expelled them from the house. This, many who have no sympathy with the tenets of the Remonstrants, may consider to have been an act of uncalled-for severity and performed in a harsh manner by the President.

The Synod now proceeded to examine the doctrines of the Remonstrants as contained in their writings and their communications to the Synod and they pronounced them to be neither according to the Scriptures nor the Confession of Faith. The Canons, expressing the judgment of the Synod on the five controverted heads of doctrine were now framed, discussed, modified, and finally adopted with entire unanimity. Their moderate statement of the Calvinistic doctrines commended them to the differing parties of which the Synod was composed, of Supra lapsarians and Infra lapsarians alike and every member affixed his name to them. We have often read them, and always with increased admiration of their clear, beautiful and Scriptural statements on the disputed points, as well as of the pious and reverent spirit that pervades them. The question, who were the more blamable in this controversy, is of little importance to us, compared with the question whether the conclusions arrived at are in accordance with the Word of God.

The Heidelberg Catechism and the Confession of Faith were reviewed and confirmed; and it was resolved, that thenceforth all ministers, all candidates for the ministry, and all schoolmasters should subscribe them. A large committee of learned divines was appointed to make a new translation of the Scriptures into the Dutch language directly from the original tongues. After the labors of eighteen years a version singularly faithful, excellent in every respect, and accompanied with most valuable annotations was issued, and which is known as the States Bible.* The Rules of Church Government which had been adopted by previous synods, were now reviewed, amendments and additions were made, and they were formed into a more complete system. To the liturgical forms were added, one for the baptism of adults, two prayers to be used, one at the opening, and the other at the close of the meetings of the consistory, and one at the meeting of the deacons. Just before the close of the Synod, the committee on the revision of its acts was authorized to join the liturgical to the other public writings. The settlement of the

---

*Post Acta, Sess. 178. Hinlopen's Nederlandsche Overzetting des Bybels. Rev. Dr. T. W. Chambers' Art. on States Bible in Ref. Ch. Quarterly, July, 1880.

Church order, and of the Liturgy will be more fully treated in subsequent chapters.

Judgment was passed on the cited ministers. They were pronounced innovators and disturbers of the Church and Nation, obstinate and rebellious; leaders of faction; teachers of false doctrine and workers of schism; and were deprived of their offices both ecclesiastical and academical, till such time as they had satisfied the Church with evident signs of repentance.* The cases of such Remonstrant ministers as had not been before the Synod were committed to the provincial synods and classes to be dealt with prudently, patiently, and yet firmly.

Thus ended this famous Synod whose "marvelous labors," President Bogerman declared in his closing address, had made "hell tremble." Some men have been unable to find words strong enough to express their abhorrence of the acts of this Synod, while others have declared that the church of Holland stood at the head of the Churches of Christendom, when at Dordrecht she bore the most complete and glorious testimony to the grace of Jesus Christ, that man has ever been vouchsafed to bear.† When the spirit that prevailed in this Synod is brought in question, some regard may be claimed for the opinion of Bishop Hall, who, in his valedictory address to the Synod, declared that no place on earth could be more like heaven; that there was none

---

* Davies, Vol. II., p. 509.

† "Quand est-ce que l'Église de Hollande a été triomphante glorieuse? Quand a-t-elle marché a la tête de toutes les Églises de la Chrétienté? C'est lorsqu'il lui fut donné de porter dans les murs de Dordrecht le plus complet, le plus magnifique témoignage qu'il ait jamais été permis aux hommes de rendre à la grâce de Jésus-Christ."—Merle D'Aubigne, cited by Vanderkemp.

in which he would rather dwell, or the remembrance of which could afford so great delight.*

The States confirmed the judgment of the Synod; forbade all assemblies of the Remonstrants; fined those who attended them; offered rewards for the apprehension of their preachers; and, in short, refused them privileges that were granted to other sects and even to infidels. Many of the deposed ministers were banished from the country. In all this we see the Republic departing from her own principles hitherto so gloriously illustrated. There can be no doubt that the Synod was justifiable in silencing those who taught contrary to the received doctrines. If the Arminians had peaceably withdrawn from the Church when they found that they could not teach her received doctrines, they would doubtless have been tolerated as a new sect. But they continued in the Church, propagating their views, and the contentions of years exasperated both parties, so that in the hour of victory toleration was forgotten. The union between the Church and State was such, that no one questioned the right and duty of the latter to uphold the former in its discipline by inflicting pains and penalties on the subjects of it.

It is pleasing to know that when Frederic Henry became Stadtholder, the banished preachers were recalled. They established churches and founded a divinity school in Amsterdam that attained considerable reputation. They have as a small sect continued in the Netherlands to the present day, but their doctrines have been widely spread and received by many ministers and members in the various Protestant Churches of the world.

"Neque enim ullus est profectò sub coelo locus aeque coeli æmulus et in quo tentorium mihi figi maluerim cujusque adeò gestiet mihi animus meminisse. Beatos verò vos quibus, hôc frui datum!" -Hall's Works, Vol. XII., p. 344.

Thus have we reached the period of the settlement of the doctrines, the polity, and the worship of the Reformed Church of the Netherlands. These she sent with her children to the New World, who came immediately after the adjournment of this famous Synod. The Rules of Government and the Liturgy have in the course of time been more or less changed, while the standards of doctrine have remained the same in every particular.

CHAPTER III.

THE PLANTING OF THE CHURCH IN AMERICA.

On the 11th of September 1609, the Half-moon a vessel of eighty tons' burden, commanded by Hendrick Hudson, passed through the Narrows and anchored in New York harbor. Hudson came under the auspices of the Dutch East India Company to seek for a north western passage to the East Indies, and sailed up the river to where Albany is now situated, and then returned. Soon other vessels were sent out, and trading posts were established at Fort Orange, now Albany, and on the island of Manhattan, now New York, in the year 1614, six years before the landing of the Pilgrims at Plymouth. In the year 1623 the permanent colonization of New Netherland was begun under the authority of the West India Company which had been formed in 1621, and to which enormous powers had been given. The majority of the first company of colonists, numbering about 30 families, were Walloons. Some of these settled at the Wallabout, Long Island, a few went to the South or Delaware river, a few to the Fresh or Connecticut river, and the largest division of them to Fort Orange, now Albany. Their object was to better their temporal condition; they came not for conscience's sake nor as fugitives from oppression, for Holland was the land of the free.

But they had a care and zeal for the Church, and provision was made as soon as practicable, for the public worship of God according to the customs of the Fatherland. Before they could have an ordained minister and full ecclesiastical services they had two "krank-besoeckers" or "comforters of the sick," Sebastian Jansen Krol and Jan Huyck, officers of the Church of Holland, appointed in 1626, to visit and pray with the sick. These met the people on Sundays in a room above a horsemill, and read the Scriptures and the creeds to them. Such was the beginning of public worship in New Amsterdam.*

On the 7th of April 1628, Jonas Michaelius, the first one of the Dutch ministers in America, arrived at New Amsterdam and immediately formed a church numbering fifty communicants, Dutch and Walloons. The director, Peter Minuit, and his brother-in-law, Jan Huyghen were chosen elders, both of whom had been church officers at Wesel on the Rhine; the former of the French congregation in that town, the latter of the Dutch. As the Walloons had an imperfect knowledge of the Dutch language, Michaelius in administering the Lord's supper to them, used the French language and followed the French mode. He expressed himself as anxious to do something for the conversion of the Indians. How long his ministry continued or how successful it was is unknown. No documents concerning him have come to light, except his own letter written seven weeks after his arrival, in which the above mentioned facts are stated.†

The next minister, Rev. Everardus Bogardus, came in the spring of 1633, accompanied by Adam Roelandsen the first school-master, for among the Dutch, the church and school went together. The church records now in existence go back to the ministry of Bogardus even to 1639.

*Brodhead, Vol. I., p. 165. Documentary History of New York, Vol. III., p. 27.
†See letter of Michaelius in Corwin's Manual, 3rd Ed., p. 2.

Mr. Bogardus married Annetje Jansen the widow
of Roelof Jansen who had been assistant superintendent of farms at Rensselaerswyck, now Albany, and from
whom the creek called Roelof Jansen's Kill, running
through Columbia Co. N. Y., and emptying into the
Hudson near Red Hook, derived its name. He obtained a
grant of sixty-two acres of land on Manhattan Island,
lying north of the present Warren street. This is
the valuable property in possession of the corporation
of Trinity Church, and to which the ten thousand heirs
of Annetje Jansen are still laying claim on the ground
of some defect in the conveyance.[*]

On account of the rapid increase of the colony, a plain
wooden building for holding church services, was put
up near the East river, on what is now Broad street,
between Pearl and Bridge streets, and near it a dwelling house and stable were built for the minister, for
it was the universal custom of the Dutch of the olden
time to have a house for the pastor as soon as they had
a church.

Of the ministry of Bogardus we have little on record ;
but, it does not seem to have been a very happy or successful one. Difficulties of some sort arose between
him and the Directors Von Twiller and Kieft, and he
thundered at them from the pulpit in language pointed,
but not always refined. His difficulty with Kieft having produced some trouble in the congregation, he
resigned in 1647, and sailed for Holland, Kieft being
a fellow-passenger. The vessel was wrecked on the
coast of Wales and they both, together with eighty
others, perished.[†]

---

[*] Brodhead. Vol. I., p. 265.—Documentary History of New
York, Vol. III., p. 27.

[†] Brodhead, Vol. I., p. 472.—Doc. Hist. IV., p. 70.

Under Kieft's administration a new church was built in the year 1642, within the walls of Fort Amsterdam, which stood on what is now called the Battery. De Vries says, that dining with the director one day, he told him that it was a shame that when the English came to Manhattan they should see only "a mean barn in which we preached. The first thing they built in New England after their dwelling houses, was a fine church ; we should do the like ; we have fine oak wood, good mountain stone, and excellent lime which we burn from oyster shells, much better than our lime in Holland. The proposal took at once with the director ; a subscription was headed by him, and church-masters were appointed to superintend the work.*

This church was seventy-two feet long, fifty wide, and sixteen high, and cost twenty-five hundred guilders, and the congregation worshiped in it until the opening of the church in Garden street in 1693. After the surrender of the colony to the English in 1664, the consistory granted the use of it, when not occupied by themselves, to the English, whose military chaplains officiated in it. Afterwards, the Rev. Mr. Vesey the first rector of Trinity parish, occupied it for one service on the Lord's Day. When the church in Garden street was opened, the Dutch abandoned the church in the fort, which then became the property of the government, took the name of King's Chapel, and continued to be used for worship by the chaplains of the garrison until its destruction by fire in 1741.†

In 1630 Kiliaen Van Rensselaer of Amsterdam, a polisher of pearls and diamonds, bought a large tract of land around Fort Orange, now Albany, and planted the colony of Rensselaerswyck over which he was

*Brodhead, Vol. I., p. 335.
†T. D. W. in the Christian Intelligence—Dec. 2, 1852.

acknowledge 1 Patroon.* In 1642 he secured the services
of a learned clergyman, Johannis Megapolensis; guaranteed him a salary and sent him out to his colony,
which at the time contained about one hundred persons.
After his arrival a parsonage was procured for him,
and soon after a church was built to the west of the
Patroon's trading house, in a pine grove near the present Church street. This first church in Albany was
thirty-four feet long, and nineteen wide, had a canopied
pulpit, pews for the magistrates and church officers,
and nine benches for the people, and accommodated
the people until 1656 at which time a new church was
begun at the intersection of State and Market streets.
An oaken pulpit was procured from Holland, for which
the people had subscribed twenty-five beavers, worth
two hundred guilders, and seventy-five were added by
the Amsterdam Chamber who also presented the congregation with a bell.†

The third church was built in 1715 around the walls
of the old one, which in the meantime continued to be
used for worship, and was removed on the completion
of the new building, worship having been omitted only
three Sundays. The coats of arms of the old Dutch
families of Albany were painted on the windows of
this church, and remained there until its demolition
in 1806. The old octagonal oak pulpit which came from
Holland and a fragment of the little bell bearing the
inscription—"Anno 1601" are still preserved by the
First Reformed Church of Albany.

Megapolensis seems to have been a most worthy and
zealous, as well as learned minister. He was one of
the first Protestant preachers to the Indians in this

---

*A Patroon was a feudal chief of territory colonized by him,
under prescribed conditions. For an account of these conditions see Broadhead, Vol. I., p. 194.

†Brodhead, Vol. I., pp. 342, 374, 624.

country, having learned their language and preached
Christ to them three or four years before John Eliot
began his labors among the Indians in the vicinity of
Boston. He took great interest in those children of the
forest who came to the fort to trade, and he wrote a
treatise about the Mohawks, which was published in
Holland. After he had served the church at Albany,
the stipulated term of six years, he started on his return
to the Fatherland. But when he reached New Amsterdam, Director Stuyvesant persuaded him to remain,
because Backerus, their minister had left, and the Province he thought, should not be left entirely without a
minister and ordinances. He especially urged the
fact, that "children were every Sunday presented for
baptism—sometimes one, sometimes two, yea, sometimes three and four together." Megapolensis yielded
and became minister of New Amsterdam in the place
of Backerus, and so remained until his death in 1670.*

After Megapolensis had left Albany, his son-in-law
Dom. Grassmere, came and preached with acceptance,
although he was under censure of the classis of Alkmaar. After two years he returned to Holland with
a view of obtaining an appointment to New Amsterdam,
in which he did not succeed. In 1652, two ministers
were sent to the Province, Samuel Drisius and Gideon
Schaats. Drisius was a man of much learning and
able to preach in Dutch, French and English; he was
appointed a colleague of Megapolensis, and occasionally
preached in French to the Huguenots who had settled
on Staten Island.† He labored in New Amsterdam until

*Brodhead v. 1., pp. 375-508.

† French Protestants formed a most important element in
the population of New Netherland. The first company of
permanent settlers was composed principally of Walloons.
The French Huguenots formed, after the Dutch, " the richest

his death which occurred in 1681, a period of twenty-
nine years. Schaats had been a schoolmaster who, having received ordination, was sent out to Rensselaerswyck. It was particularly required of him to "use
all Christian zeal to bring up both the heathen and
their children in the Christian religion." His ministry
continued forty-two years, with some interruption caused
by trouble in the congregation.

A third church was established in 1654 at Midwout,
the present Flatbush on Long Island. The people on
Long Island had thus far been compelled to travel
miles, and then cross the East river to attend public
worship. The ministers of New Amsterdam went over
occasionally and preached in private houses, but the
want of a settled pastor was so deeply felt that a committee was sent over from New Amsterdam to effect
a church organization. Providentially, just at this time
the Rev. Johannis Theodorus Polhemus arrived from
Itamarca, in Brazil, where he had been stationed; and
he was immediately employed to officiate for the new
congregation, with a view of receiving a regular appointment from Holland, the people engaging to support
him independently of the West India Company. A

and most considerable part of the population." They speedily
identified themselves with the Dutch, adopted their language,
and worshiped in their churches, though in the city of New
York they had a church of their own in which the French language was used, and in which it is continued to be used
to the present time. This is now known as the French
Church, du Saint-Esprit in 22nd Street. The Huguenots
located not only in the city, but at New Rochelle, on Long
Island, on Staten Island, at New Paltz and at Hackensack in
New Jersey, and their names are now borne by numerous
and respectable families of their descendants. See "Collection of the Huguenot Society of America Vol. I., New York,
1886."

church was immediately built in which he officiated every Sunday morning, and in the afternoon he served the people at Breuckelen and New Amersfoort or Flatlands alternately.*

Thus far there was no municipal government in New Amsterdam, but it was ruled by the Director and Council appointed by the West India Company, but the earnest petition of the people was at last granted, and in 1652, it was ordered that New Amsterdam should be organized so as to resemble Old Amsterdam as much as possible. Burgomasters and all the usual officers were appointed, and books of record were begun, and the first entry in one of them was a solemn prayer for a blessing on their undertaking.† This government had less of the elements of popular liberty than the governments of most of the towns of Holland, for undue power was left in the hands of the Director. And yet, it has been said, that whatever was known of popular liberty in New Netherland was learned from the immigrants who came thither from New England; a strange assertion in face of the fact that the people had long been earnestly pleading, not for a new thing, but for privileges which they had enjoyed in their native towns across the water, where legally qualified persons had a voice in the selection of the magistrates.

We now come to a part of the history which it is not pleasant to review—the history of persecuting measures against non-conforming sects. At the first, all were allowed, as in Holland, to enjoy their own opinions without hindrance, and New Amsterdam became like Old Amsterdam an asylum for the oppressed from

*Brodhead, Vol. I., p. 581.

†A translation of this prayer may be seen in "Valentine's History of New York."

every quarter. Francis Doughty, a minister who was
harshly treated in Massachusetts, early came to New
Netherland and a grant of land at Mispath, now New-
town, L. I., and many privileges were given him. John
Throgmorton, driven from Massachusetts with Roger
Williams, came with his friends to Westchester. Lady
Moody, an Anabaptist, excommunicated in New England, settled at Gravesend, L. I. There were also at
various places some Presbyterians, Independents, and
Baptists who dwelt in peace among the Dutch until
jealousies were excited, and Stuyvesant, as a defender of
the Church, issued a proclamation against all who should
" hold conventicles not in harmony with the established
religion." Heavy fines were exacted from all who trans-
gressed. The West India Company being appealed to,
rebuked Stuyvesant for his intolerance and commanded
him " to allow to all the free exercise of religion in their
own houses."*

The Lutherans in New Amsterdam had, in 1654, asked
permission of Director Stuyvesant to have a minister
of their own and separate public worship, but their petition was denied. In 1657, the Lutheran congregation
of Amsterdam sent over a minister, John Ernestus
Goetwater, without having consulted the Classis or the
West India Company. His arrival created great
excitement and he was at once ordered to return; but
this order was not enforced because of the state of his
health. The West India Company doubtless feeling
that due respect had not been paid to them, approved
of what had been done in the case, though they thought
that it " might have been performed in a more gentle
way." The desire and policy of the company were
to draw the Lutherans into the Reformed Church, and

---

*Brodhead, Vol. I., p. 617.

as the chief objection of the Lutherans was to the formulary used in baptism, the Directors sent orders to the ministers not to be too precise in this matter, but to use the old formulary which had been framed in Reformation times, and which would satisfy the Lutherans. The ministers sent back a letter in which they defended their cause, and asked for help in the ministry.*

Some Quakers also who, being driven from New England, had come hither for rest were subjected to various annoyances and persecutions.

In reviewing these proceedings it is but just to say that persecution did not occur under any one of the four governors who preceded Stuyvesant, and that the municipal government of New Amsterdam had nothing to do with these acts that occurred under his administration. It was the work of the provincial government, which was composed of the Director and Council, who were not the representatives of the people, as were the officers of the city government. Moreover, all intolerant measures ceased at once by order of the Directors of the West India Company, so that neither these Directors, nor the popular municipal government were responsible for these departures from the Holland principle of toleration. "It is our opinion," wrote the Directors to Stuyvesant, that at least the consciences of men ought to remain free and unshackled. Let every one remain free as long as he is modest, moderate, his political conduct irreproachable, and as long as he does

*Brodhead, Vol. I., p. 642. Letter of Drisius and Megapolensis, Doc. Hist. of New York, Vol. III., p. 69. The Lutherans scrupled at the enquiry "if they believe that the doctrine which is preached in that congregation, in unison with the Synod of Dort is the true one." Albany Records; Translations Vol. IV., p. 267.

not offend others or oppose the government. This maxim of moderation has always been the guide of our magistrates in this city (Amsterdam) and the consequence has been that people have flocked from every land to this asylum. Tread thus in their steps, and we doubt not you will be blessed."*

The earnest request that more ministers might be sent to meet the growing wants of the Province was favorably answered by the Directors, who, in 1660, sent Rev. Hermanus Blom and Rev. Henricus Selyns. The former came with a wide commission "to preach both on water and on the land, and in all the neighborhood, but principally in Esopus." He was the first minister of what was then called Wiltwyck, Indian village or Esopus, now Kingston New York, a settlement that suffered much from attacks by the Indians.† Selyns settled at Brenckelen, then a village containing thirty-one families and one hundred and thirty-four persons, where he conducted services in a barn until a church edifice was completed. As the people of Brenckelen were not able to give him an adequate support, Selyns was engaged by Governor Stuyvesant to officiate on Sunday afternoons at a chapel which he had built some distance out of town, on his bouwerie or farm, whence we have the name of the street Bowery. Although this chapel was far away, and there were woods and hills between, yet many people went out to attend evening service there; and here, also, some forty negroes, living in the vicinity received religious instruction.‡

*Brodhead, Vol. I., p. 707.

† Doc. Hist. Vol. III., p. 581.

‡ St. Mark's church in Ninth street stands on this spot where also Gov. Stuyvesant was buried. Peter Stuyvesant Esq., a great-grandson of the Governor, gave in 1793, to the corporation of Trinity Church the ground for the erection of this building.

Polhemus retired from Breuckelen on the arrival of Selyns and confined his labors to Flatbush and Flatlands.*

About this time, Bergen in New Jersey was settled, and the ministers of New Amsterdam for many years went over occasionally on Mondays to conduct public worship and administer the sacraments, for their own people required their services on the Lord's day. The voorleser always conducted the worship on the Lord's day in the Bergen church, except when some minister happened to be in the neighborhood. This practice was certainly continued to the year 1751, for in that year Rev. Gualterus Du Bois, while preparing for such a visit, was seized with the disease which, in a few days terminated his life. The first pastor of the church of Bergen was Rev. William Jackson, who was installed September 10th, 1757.†

In 1654, a church was organized by Polhemus on his way from Brazil at New Amstel, a colony established by the City of Amsterdam on the South or Delaware river, now New Castle, Del. Rev. Everardus Welius "a young man of much esteem in life, in studies, in gifts, and in conversation, ministered to this colony from 1657 to 1659 when he died. Being far distant from the other Dutch Churches, it early joined the Presbyterian body.

In 1664, Samuel, son of Rev. Johannis Megapolensis, having studied at the University of Utrecht, and been ordained in Holland, returned to take the place of Selyns who now returned to Holland. He was also a doctor of medicine, a young man of much learning and excellent judgment. Such confidence was reposed in him that he was appointed one of the commissioners to treat with Nicolls, the British commander, about the surrender

*Letter of Selyns. Doc. Hist. Vol. III. p. 72.
†Doc. Hist. Vol. III.. p. 324.

of the city which took place on the 8th day of September 1664.

Gov. Stuyvesant protested that he would "much
rather be carried out dead" than consent to a surrender,
but he yielded to the importunity of the city authorities. Megapolensis saw to it that the rights of the Dutch
Church should not be impaired by the surrender.
Among the articles of capitulation was one guaranteeing
to the Dutch "liberty of their consciences in Divine worship and Church discipline," and besides, they were to
be allowed their own customs concerning inheri-
tances, and some other privileges were allowed them.*

Thus ended the Dutch rule in Manhattan with the
exception of the brief restoration in 1673. From the
time of the establishment of the first trading station
to the surrender was about fifty years, and from the
organization of the church by Michaelius in 1628, thirty-
six years. The city contained at the time of the surrender about fifteen hundred inhabitants; in the entire
Province, there were eleven churches and seven ministers.

At this point the first period of the history of the
Reformed Dutch Church in North America ceases. The
Church was as a grain of mustard seed when Dutch rule
and immigration ceased, and governmental care and
patronage passed away forever.

*Brodhead, Vol. I., p. 762.

CHAPTER IV.

THE DEVELOPMENT OF THE CHURCH TO FINAL INDE-PENDENCE.

The development and progress of the Church for one hundred and twenty-eight years after the surrender of New Netherland to the English went on gradually in the face of great and diversified difficulties. Four generations had to pass away before the Dutch churches in America attained to an independent, organized existence as one body. This chapter will be largely occupied with an account of these difficulties and of their removal. Our space does not allow of such enlargement on these as is desirable, and we must compress in a few pages matters to which a volume might well be devoted. It is well known that the Reformed Church of the Netherlands has not become one of the leading denominations in this land.

Various reasons for this have been readily discovered by candid and reflecting people, but the unthinking have contented themselves with attributing it to the slowness of the past generations of Dutchmen, and to their lack of a liberal and progressive spirit. They can see no other reason why the first Church that was planted in the metropolis of the new world should not now cover the face of the whole land. It is thought that she should at least have maintained her position as the leading Church in the city of New York. We are not disposed to excuse any lack of progressive spirit in the past generations, but let us at the same time judge intelligently and fairly. Until the period of the Revolution, and for some time afterward, this Church labored in common with others under difficulties which arose from the circumstances of the country which was new, with resources undeveloped, and a population struggling to make a livelihood. But she also encountered difficulties that were peculiar to herself and were mighty barriers to her progress. When we understand them we will not wonder that she is at this day small, but rather that she has an existence in the land.

In the year 1664, the province of New Netherland was surrendered to the English. At that time there were, as we have seen, only eleven congregations and seven ministers in the whole province. The infant Church was now deprived of all help and patronage from the civil power, for the governor and authorities belonged, thenceforth to the Church of England, and of course, gave to that Church all their influence. Still, the mass of the population was Dutch, as were also the most wealthy and respectable inhabitants, and the Reformed Dutch Church continued to be for a long time the most prominent Church in the city and the province. Though the Dutch immigration virtually ceased, some new congregations were formed within a few years after the surrender, along the Hudson and in New Jersey, also one at Schenectady and one on Staten Island. Some of these churches had no ministers, and the services on the Lord's day were usually conducted by the voorleser. Occasionally they were visited by pastors of other churches who administered Baptism and the Lord's Supper.

The change of government was a detriment to the Dutch Church not only through the loss of prestige and patronage, but also through positive inimical influences exerted by those who were in authority. The

royal governors acted on the idea that the English Episcopal Church must necessarily be the Church by law
established in the English colonies, as well as in the
mother country, and this led to many aggressive and
oppressive acts. In 1693, under the administration
of Gov. Fletcher, who was a very zealous Episcopalian, an act of Assembly was passed providing for the
settlement and support of ministers in the four principal counties of the province; New York, Westchester,
Queens and Richmond. It was provided by this act
that a certain number of vestry-men and church-war-
dens should be annually chosen in each county by the
free-holders, that they should have authority to choose
ministers for the parishes, and to levy a tax upon all
the inhabitants for their support. It is true that the
act did not require the ministers to be Episcopalians,
and a subsequent act declared that dissenters (so called)
might be elected, but it was so managed that Episcopalians were always chosen. The Dutch people had their
own regularly organized churches and ministers and
they could not be expected to take a very active part
in such novel proceedings. So it happened that until
the Declaration of Independence, the people of all
denominations in the counties mentioned were compelled to support the ministers of the Episcopal Church
as well as their own. This caused no little trouble in
several congregations, and resulted in the removal of
many excellent families, especially from Long Island,
to the valley of the Raritan and other parts of New
Jersey.

The injustice of this act in its practical workings was
manifest, for the Episcopalians were a small body composed principally of persons connected with the government, while the Dutch embraced the great mass of
permanent settlers in the country. The testimony of

Chief Justice Lewis Morris, given in a letter to the secretary of the "Society for the propagation of the Gospel in foreign parts" is valuable on this point, for he was an Episcopalian in authority.

He says, "The act to settle the Church is very loosely worded, which, as things stood then, when it was made, could not be avoided, the dissenters claiming the benefit of it as well as we; and the act, without such wresting, will admit a construction in their favor as well as ours. They think it was intended for them, and that they only have a right to it. There is no comparison in our numbers, and they can, on the death of the incumbents, call persons of their own persuasion in every place but the city of New York; and if by force the salary is taken from them, and paid to the minister of the Church (Episcopalian) it may be the means of subsisting these ministers, but they wont make many converts among a people who think themselves very much injured."

He then suggests that it would have been better to pass no act, but to work quietly with the youth, since the adult English population in the province was not very promising material. Our eastern friends will appreciate the compliment paid by a high-churchman to their fathers when he says, "For as New England, excepting some families, was the scum of the old, so the greatest part of the English in this province was the scum of the new, who brought as many opinions, almost as persons, but neither religion nor virtue, and have acquired a very little since." *

Very vigorous measures were employed for the spread and establishment of the Episcopal Church. The "Society for the propagation of the Gospel in foreign

*Documentary History, Vol. III., p. 150.

parts" sent over many missionaries, who laid the foundations of Episcopal Churches in the colonies. Unpopular, as the act for settling the Church may have been, when its first workings were seen, yet we must remember that it continued in force more than eighty years; that new generations came up under it, who could not have the feeling against it that the old had cherished; that all who looked for patronage or office went into the Episcopal Church; that those who desired to move in court society were attracted to that Church; and also, that many doubtless drew their decisive argument from their pockets and concluded to worship in a Church which they were compelled to support, and to abandon the Church of their fathers. We ought not to be surprised to learn that many Dutch families, especially in the city of New York, found their way into the Episcopal Church.

Another cause not only produced much internal trouble, but was an effectual hindrance to progress; that is, the continued exclusive use of the Dutch language in public worship. As long as this barrier remained, the country was not open to the Church, and she could not pass beyond the bounds of the Dutch settlements. She could grow only by the natural increase of the Dutch population, for the immigration from Holland was arrested, and she could not bring into her fold, strangers of Presbyterian and Calvinistic views, because she spoke what was to them an unknown tongue. The country was English, and it rapidly filled up with people who used the English tongue. The language of the laws and courts and schools was English. Intermarriages took place between the English and Dutch, and the English language was used in the adjacent colonies. Nothing therefore could be done for the extension of the church, and there was a certainty that it must lose ground within its original limits, for the young people, especially in the city, were losing the language of their fathers. Many who could use the colloquial language of the family with its limited vocabulary, could not understand the very different phraseology used in preaching and public worship, for their school instruction and reading were in English. There was also a growing predilection for the English language, for it became fashionable and many of the weaker ones were ashamed of being suspected of an ability even to understand their mother tongue.

Of course, there was an urgent and increasing demand for the introduction of the English language into the public services of the Church, and a formal petition for it had been presented to the consistory of the church in New York city at an early day. The subject was seriously discussed and the sagacious could not fail to see that the continued existence of the Church depended on it. But the proposal met with strong opposition, especially from the aged members, who were ardently attached to their language, and really thought that if they should part with it, the essentials of the Church would be lost. The controversy raised by this question in the church of New York was most bitter and violent, and she lost immensely by it. In the first place, she lost those who desired the introduction of English and were impatient of the delay; in the second place, she lost the lovers of peace, who sought refuge from the strife, in other communions; and in the third place, when English was introduced, she lost the uncompromising opposers of it, who were determined never to hear it in the church of their fathers.

The step had to be taken. The consistory, after due consideration, resolved to call one minister to preach and catechise in English, while his three colleagues

should continue to officiate in Dutch. They proceeded
very cautiously and judiciously in making this moderate beginning. In order to prove that they were not, as
was charged, secretly hostile to the Dutch they resolved,
if possible, to get an English preacher from Holland,
and from the Classis of Amsterdam. They sent a
blank call to the Classis, which was filled by that body
with the name of Archibald Laidlie, a Scotchman and
minister of the English Church in Flushing, on the island
of Walcheren, in Zealand. He arrived in New York in
the spring of 1764 and preached his first sermon on the
15th of April from the text, which he announced in
both Dutch and English, 2 Cor. v : 11. "Knowing therefore the terror of the Lord we persuade men." It was
in the Middle Dutch Church, corner of Nassau and
Cedar streets, and a very numerous congregation, including the Mayor and some of the Aldermen of the city
were present. But they were not yet prepared for the
innovation of singing the praises of God, in a language
strange to their assemblies. The voorleser Jacobus
Van Antwerp after having read a chapter in English,
started the familiar sonorous strains of the Dutch mel-
ody. It was with many a day of great rejoicing. "Ah !
Domine," said some pious, praying people to him at the
close of a prayer meeting, "we offered up many an
earnest prayer in Dutch for your coming among us,
and truly the Lord has heard us in English, and has sent
you to us."

A better man than Dr. Laidlie, for the position at the
time, could not have been selected. He was a man of
learning, of eminent piety, excellent judgment and
peaceful disposition. He overcame the prejudices of
many, who were won by the kind and affectionate
deportment of the "English minister." He was a faithful preacher, was warmly attached to the standards and

usages of the Church, and his ministry was greatly blessed. During the Revolutionary war he retired to Redhook N. Y., where he died in 1778.*

The members of the Dutch party were very persevering in their opposition. They rejected the liberal offers of the consistory, they remonstrated, they put obstacles in the way of Dr. Laidlie, and attempted to change the old mode of electing members of the consistory. The elders and deacons had always chosen their successors and published their names on three successive Sabbaths for the approval of the congregation; but the Dutch party supposing themselves to be in the majority, claimed that all the members in full communion were entitled to vote, and should vote at the next election. To test the question, one came to the election and offered his vote which was rejected, and then a civil suit was brought, which was decided in favor of the consistory. Meanwhile the congregation was canvassed, and it was ascertained that a large majority of the members was in favor of the consistory. After the decision of the case by the court, the most headstrong declared, that "if it must be English it should be English," and went to the Episcopal Church, where they never heard a syllable of the language for which they had so earnestly contended, and which they might have continued to hear until their dying day. The rest continued quietly to attend the Dutch sevice in the old church in Garden street until the year 1803, when the Rev. Dr. G. A. Kuypers officiated for the last time in that language.†

*The Magazine of the Reformed Dutch Church contains (Vol. II., p. 33) a memoir of Dr. Laidlie, large portions of his first sermon in New York (Vol. II., p. 161) and an interesting account of the services of the occasion on which it was delivered, given by one who was present. (Vol. III. p. 24.)

†See Remonstrance and Answer in Documentary History of New York, Vol. III., p. 308. Also Gunn's Life of Livingston. p. 99.

Unquestionably, these people were ardently attached to their Church, but they grievously mistook her true policy. They loved their own language, the language in which their fathers had worshiped, and in which their mothers' earliest words of affection had been spoken. They were not required to abandon it, but only to consent to the introduction of the English for the benefit of those who preferred it. The sacrifice of prejudice and feeling should have been cheerfully made, and the measures of the consistory have been quietly submitted to.

This was a great era in the history of the Church in America, but we must not mistake its nature by dating the cessation of the Dutch language in public worship from this time. This was only the beginning of a very gradual introduction of the English, by the calling of one English preacher to the church of New York. Even in that church, the Dutch continued in use for some time, and in many country congregations for years. Gradually, both languages came to be used in alternate services, until a little more than half a century ago the Dutch was no more heard in public worship. Since that time, a few aged ministers were accustomed to deliver one address at the Lord's table, and occasionally to lecture in private houses in the Dutch language for the benefit of the few representatives left of the past generations. The last service in the Middle Dutch Church of New York, after it was leased to the General Government for a Post-office, was held August 11th, 1844, and the vast assembly composed, in a great measure of those who had there been baptized and made confession of their faith, was dismissed by the Rev. Dr. Thomas DeWitt with the Apostolic Benediction in the venerable language in which the building had been dedicated, and in which the pastors had for many years ministered. It was beautifully appropriate that this tribute should be paid to the Dutch language in the edifice within whose walls the first English sermon had been preached. Thus, gradually did the mother language of the Church depart, lingering to the last in the affections of those who loved it for the sake of the fathers, and of the memories of childhood. The minutes of the General Synod began to be kept in English in the year 1794, and so it became the official language of the Church; and this, it seems, scarcely credible to us, was done less than a hundred years ago, and after the Dutch had had more than a century and a half of undisputed sway.*

Another very serious hindrance to the progress of the Church, was the fact that there was no regular provision in this country for the education and ordination of ministers. Of course the first ministers had to come from Holland, and whenever one was needed by a church, application was made to the directors of the West India Company, who for the most part resided in Amsterdam. They consulted with the ministers of that city, and usually left it with them to procure a man suited to the field and willing to enter it. Having found such a man, he was ordained by the Classis of Amsterdam and sent out by the company. After the cessation of the Dutch rule, the churches in America corresponded directly with the Classis, to which their interests had been committed by the Synod of North Holland, and they were by it supplied with ministers. So it happened, that for many years all the ministers

*The Holland brethren in the West brought their language with them, and they, of course, use it in public worship. But wiser than our fathers were, they have adopted the enlightened policy of favoring the introduction of the English into their churches as soon as the general good demands it.

and churches of the denomination in America were subject to the Classis of Amsterdam. The voluminous and valuable correspondence between this classis and the churches and ministers of this country is in possession of the General Synod, and it is hoped that it will ere long be given to the public in an English translation. That Classis has always been noted for the interest it has taken in churches in the Dutch colonies in the East and West Indies as well as on the American continent. It also planted the German Reformed Church in this country by commissioning and supporting the first German ministers in the state of Pennsylvania.*

The dependence of the American Churches on Holland which in the early period of their history was absolutely necessary, and highly useful, became in time the occasion of damage; for many failed to see when the time of minority had ceased, and the time for independent life and action had come.. The inevitable result was the formation of two parties, a progressive and a conservative one causing strife, agitation, delay, weakness and loss. The inconveniences of the situation were numerous, great and obvious. There was no higher judicatory in the country than a consistory, and consequently no power of ordination, and so ministers had to be procured from Holland, and persons desiring the ministry were obliged to go thither to receive ordination. Much time was lost and much expense incurred in the settlement of ministers, and many congregations remained vacant a long time, and some were never supplied with pastors. Discipline could not be promptly and thoroughly exercised, for a minister could be tried only by the classis and all courts of appeal from the

*Proceedings of the German Coetus MS.

acts of consistories were on the other side of the water. These and other difficulties made it impossible for the Church to hold her own, to say nothing of extending herself. No attempt to change the order of things was made until the year 1737.

In that year a few ministers, keenly feeling these inconveniences, met together in the city of New York, and, encouraged by the Classis of Amsterdam, devised a plan of an organization for fraternal conference on the state and wants of the churches. This plan was submitted to the churches and it was approved by them; it was then adopted by a second convention of ministers and elders in 1738, and was finally sent to the Classis of Amsterdam for its approbation, which was given nine years later, in 1747.*

It is presumed that the Classis, on further thought of the matter, concluded that they had been too hasty, and that they were liable to endanger their prerogative, for the next year (1739) they wrote to some parties that they would consent to a coetus, "under the express condition that care was taken not to have a word uttered against the doctrine, and to have no preparatory or final examinations for candidates or minis-

---

* The members of the second convention, which met in the Consistory Chamber, New York, April 27th, 1738, were:

MINISTERS.	ELDERS.	
Gualterus DuBois,	Antony Rutgers, Abram Lefferts,	For New York.
Bernardus Freeman,	Pieter Nevius, Dirk Brinkerhoff,	Long Eyland.
Cornelius Van Santvoort,	Goosse Adriansse, Staten Eyland.	
T. J. Frilinghuizen,	H. Fisscher, Raretans.	
Reinhard Erigson,	J. Zutveen, Nauwessinks.	
A. Curtenius,	— Saboriski, Hakkinzak.	
J. Böhm,	Ryts Snyder, Philadelphia.	
G. Haeghoort,	F. Van Dyk, Second River.	
J. Schüler,	J. Spies, Schoogharie.	

ters; these being matters which were, by the Synod of Dort, restricted to the respective classes, and which, therefore, were reserved by us, in forming a coetus some years since in the colony of Surinam."

This body, called the Coetus, organized in 1747, had no ecclesiastical authority, but was merely advisory. Consequently all the evils that we have mentioned continued to exist, and indeed were felt more keenly than ever. In a few special cases the Coetus was at first permitted by the Classis to ordain ministers. This tended to open the eyes of the ministers and people to see that the churches in this country were competent to do their own work, and that there was no reason why they should not be allowed to do it. They saw, also, that the ministers who had been taught and ordained in America were no less able and useful than many who had come from Holland.

The demand for the formation of a classis was now openly made, and in 1754, it was proposed in the Coetus that that body should be made a regular classis, and that the opinions of the churches upon the matter should be obtained, so that it might be brought favorably before the Synod of North Holland. This action was taken with great unanimity, and yet, before the churches could be consulted, bitter opposition to it unexpectedly sprang up. The matter was never brought before the Synod of North Holland, and the failure of the movement was the signal for a bitter war of parties in this country that was carried on for fifteen years.

While all seemed to be desirous that some way might be provided for the education and ordination of ministers in this country, yet they differed in their views about methods. Under the leadership of Dom. Ritzema, of New York city, a strong and successful effort was made, to secure a clause in the charter of King's (Columbia) College of New York authorizing the establishment in that college of a Professorship of Divinity for the Dutch churches. But this proved to be unsatisfactory on account of the conditions connected with it. It was earnestly opposed by those who were known as the coetus party, who immediately took the bold step of converting the Coetus into an independent classis by which nine persons were in time, inducted into the ministry; and also of beginning measures for the establishment of a literary and theological institution independent of the existing neighboring colleges.

The ministers who were natives of the country, and especially those who had been ordained here, generally favored the Coetus, as did their churches. Vacant congregations who desired ministers, but could not have them because of the trouble, delay and expense of sending to Holland for them favored it. The minds of many were influenced by seeing that some of the Holland ministers did not suit their fields of labor, and that the characters of some were not above reproach. It seemed also to be a humiliating, as well as unnecessary thing to be ever dependent on and subordinate to a foreign Church.

On the other hand some of the older ministers, who had been born and educated in Holland, and who still regarded it as their home, were bitterly opposed to the measure. They seemed to think that an ordination could hardly be valid unless it came from the Classis of Amsterdam. They feared that the Church in America would be unable to support an institution that could meet the requirements, and so she would lose her learned and respected ministry. A few of these came together in 1755, called themselves the Conferentie, and opened a correspondence with the Classis of Amsterdam in which they complained bitterly of the efforts made by the members of the Coetus, for ecclesiastical independence, and for their assumption of it in the matter of examinations and ordinations.*

It has been said that most of the learning was with the Conferentie, while practical piety, zeal and a progressive spirit were more conspicuous among the members of the Coetus. The latter naturally increased in strength daily, while the other decreased. Concerning this controversy another has said: "the peace of the churches was destroyed. Not only neighboring ministers and congregations were at variance, but in many places the same congregation was divided; and in those instances in which the members or the influential characters on different sides were nearly equal, the consequences became very deplorable. Houses of worship were locked by one part of the congregation against the other. Tumults on the Lord's day at the doors of the churches were frequent. Quarrels respecting the services and the contending claims of different ministers and people often took place. Preachers were sometimes assaulted in the pulpits, and public worship either disturbed or terminated by violence. In these attacks the conferentie party were considered as the most vehement and outrageous. But on both sides a furious and intemperate zeal prompted many to excesses which were a disgrace to the Christian name, and threatened to bring into contempt that cause which both professed to be desirous of supporting.†

*The Ministers who came together in "Conferentie" in New York, Sept. 30th, 1755; who were a minority of the old Coetus, and who at that time wrote their first letter to the Classis of Amsterdam, in which they expressed their dissatisfaction with the proceedings of the Coetus party, were Gerard Haeghoort, Anth. Curtenius, J. Ritzema, Lamb. De Ronde Benj. Van der Linde.

†Christian's Magazine, Vol. II., p. 10.

Yet, in all this strife, there was an educational process. It prepared the churches for the inevitable issue, the establishment of ecclesiastical independence. Already, all parties, Classis, Coetus, Conferentie were agreed in the general idea that in some way a ministry must be raised up in America for the American churches, and that an educational institution must be provided for the purpose. But what should that institution be? The Coetus advocated an independent, denominational college which should be entirely under the control of the Dutch people, and in which the classics, philosophy &c., should be taught as well as divinity. The Conferentie, or at least the active members of it, wished to establish a professorship of divinity in connection with the already existing King's College, and which was under the control of another denomination. The Classis of Amsterdam expressed itself as ready to fall in with any plan that might be agreed upon, but could do nothing so long as the parties here were so widely divided. It is usually thought that the Conferentie were opposed to the introduction of theological education here, which is not the case. They considered that the Coetus was transcending its powers, and was without lawful warrant, assuming the prerogatives of the Classis by examining and ordaining men. They claimed that they would agree to the making of candidates and ministers here, "if there were the same instruction in studies as in the Fatherland." In fact Ritzema's movement for the establishment of a professorship of divinity for the Dutch in King's College stimulated Frelinghuysen to his zealous efforts for the founding of an independent College.*

The Coetus party pursued their object with great energy and perseverance, and obtained from Gov. Wil-

---

*Centennial of the Theol. Seminary Appendix p. 315.

liam Franklin, of New Jersey, a charter for Queen's College dated Nov. 10th, 1766. The College did not go into operation under this charter, because of serious defects in it, and consequently a new one was obtained dated March 20th, 1770, in which the object was declared to be to supply the Dutch churches with an "able, learned, and well-qualified ministry." This did not help toward a reconciliation of the parties.*

In some of the churches, troubles arose from the aversion of many to close and faithful experimental preaching. Some of the old ministers valued orthodoxy more than experimental religion, and many members were admitted to the Church, who gave little evidence of piety. This was contrary to what was positively enjoined by the Synod of Dort. It followed, that they who knew nothing of the life of God in the soul could not endure searching preaching addressed to the conscience. Faithful, pointed preaching was one of the causes of the serious difficulties between Dom. Hermanus Meier and the Church of Kingston, N. Y. Other causes, springing from his sympathy with the Coetus party, led the Consistory to invite a conclave of neighboring ministers, who without authority, suspended him for six weeks from his ministry, and, following this action, the Consistory refused to pay his salary and declared the pulpit vacant.* The Rev. Theodorus Jacobus Frelinghuysen settled on the Raritan in 1720 and labored over the

*Centennial of the Theol, Seminary Appendix p. 332.

*The Christian's Magazine Vol. II., p. 10. The Magazine of the Reformed Dutch Church, Vol. III., p. 300, 380, contains interesting communications on the history of the Kingston difficulties. After his removal to Pompton, N. J., Dr. Meier was appointed by the General Synod Instructor in Sacred languages, and he was subsequently made a Lector or assistant Professor of Theology.

region now covered by the Reformed Churches of Somerset and adjacent counties. His faithful Evangelical ministry excited severe opposition. But he accomplished an excellent work, for religion was greatly revived in that portion of the country before the arrival of Whitfield and the Tennents with whom he was afterwards associated.*

To moderate and reflecting men, the church seemed to be on the very brink of ruin, and they saw no earthly help. Many fled from their ecclesiastical homes to find that peace among strangers which was denied them by their kindred.

God's eye, however, was upon the Church and He wrought for her a wonderful deliverance. His chosen instrument was John H. Livingston, a descendant of the eminent John Livingston of Ancram in Scotland, under one sermon of whom, at the Kirk of Shotts, five hundred souls were awakened; and who afterward found an asylum from persecution in Rotterdam where he preached and died. Robert Livingston, the son of this eminent man of God, obtained a patent for the Manor of Livingston, Columbia Co., N. Y., in 1684. John Henry, his great-grandson was born near Poughkeepsie in 1746, was graduated from Yale College in 1762, entered on the study of law, but after his conversion he devoted himself to the ministry. Having duly weighed the claims of the Episcopal, the Presbyterian, and the Reformed Dutch Churches, he determined to enter the last mentioned, of which his parents were members. He did this at the most gloomy period of her history.

*" He was a great blessing to the Dutch Church in America. He came over from Holland in the year 1720 and settled on the Raritan. He left five sons, all ministers, and two daughters married to ministers. The Christian's Magazine, Vol. II., p. 4. Dr. Messler's Historical Sketches.

He went to Holland, studied at the University of Utrecht, and returned in 1771, a Doctor of Divinity, and a minister ordained by the Classis of Amsterdam, on a call to be one of the collegiate pastors of the church in New York to officiate in the English language.

Before his departure to Holland, he was deeply affected by the state of the Church, and he had an ardent desire to become an instrument for restoring peace and harmony. Impressed with the idea that God would use him for that purpose, he as soon as he reached Holland, began to talk with ministers and others about the condition of things in America, the progress of society, and the needs of the Church. He found them for the most part well-disposed and ready to approve any feasible plan for the reconciliation of the parties, that might be proposed.

The Classis of Amsterdam, to whom the Synod of North Holland had given full powers to act as a permanent committee on the affairs of the American Churches, wrote a letter in 1768 to both the Coetus and Conferentie, proposing the establishment of a professorship of divinity in connection with Princeton College, to which both parties objected. The letter was conceived in a most admirable spirit as the following sentences show :

" Behold, dearly-beloved brethren, how the Classis is ready to lay aside its dignity, and see whether this effort may not by God's blessing, become the means of uniting in sincere love the sadly-divided brethren, who are one with us in the Reformed worship and doctrine. Oh ! that a pitifully wasted Babel might be changed into a true Philadelphia."* Nothing could be farther from the truth than the idea commonly entertained that a persistent determination on the part of the church

---

*See this letter in the Appendix to the " Centennial of the Theological Seminary," p. 334.

authorities in Holland to retain the control of the American churches was the cause of their difficulties, or, at least, of delay in their removal. On the contrary, the parties in America were chiefly at fault, and their dissensions grieved the Classis of Amsterdam, which was ready at any time to give them the right to license and ordain ministers, and to manage their own affairs when they should agree among themselves, and when independence should not involve the loss of an educated ministry, in the time to come.

The result of deliberations and conferences in Holland was the preparation and approval by the Classis of Amsterdam and the Synod of North Holland of a plan of union for the American churches. This was followed by correspondence by Mr. Livingston and others with influential members of both parties in this country. The members of the Coetus, of course, would not object, and those of the Conferentie were disposed to listen to anything that came from Holland. Some of the old issues had been removed, the bitter spirit that had prevailed had worn away, and many, tired of strife were ready for conditions of peace.

Shortly after his settlement in New York, Dr. Livingston induced the Consistory to invite all the ministers of the Dutch churches in the country, with an elder from each church, to meet in a convention to devise measures of peace and union. This invitation came from the best source possible, for the church of New York was not only a city church, the oldest, largest and most influential in the country; but it, like the church of Albany, had remained neutral in the controversy. The invitation was cordially responded to, and on the 15th of October, 1771, the convention, composed of twenty two ministers and twenty four elders met in New York. Dr. Livingston was chosen president of the convention, and it was evident at the opening of the session that the members had come together in a proper spirit and were prepared for union.

A committee of twelve, composed of two ministers and two elders from each of the parties, and the same number of neutrals, was appointed to prepare a plan of union.

Dr. Livingston being on the committee, now produced the plan which he had brought with him from Holland, and which had there been informally approved. It had three objects in view: First, to provide for the internal arrangement and government of the churches by the organization of superior church judicatories and also for the establishment of a professorship of divinity, and for the founding of schools. Second,

---

* This Convention was composed of the following members:

CHURCHES.	MINISTERS.	ELDERS.
Poughkeepsie and Fishkill,	Isaac Rysdyk.	Richard Snediker.
English Neighborhood,	Gerrit Leydekker,	Michael Moore.
Kings Co., Long Island,	{ Joannes Casp. Rubel, { Ulpianus Van Sinderen,	Englebert Lott. J. Rappelje.
New Brunswick,	Joannes Leydt,	Hendrick Visscher.
Hackensack & Schraalenberg,	Warmoldus Kuypers,	Garret de Marest.
Catskill and Coxsackie,	Joannes Schuneman.	
Bergen and Staten Island.	William Jackson,	Abram Sikkels.
Kingston,	Hermanus Meyer,	
Marbletown and Mombacus,	Dirk Romeyn.	Levi Pawling.
Millstone and Neshanic,	Joannes M. Van Harlingen,	
		Jacobus Van Arsdalen.
Gravesend and Harlem,	Martinus Schoonmaker,	Johannes Sikkels.
Hackensack & Schraalenberg,	Joannes Henricus Goetschius,	
		{ Peter Zabriskie. { Daniel Herring.
Paramus,	Benjamin Van der Linde,	Stephen Zabriskie.
Old Raritan,	Jacob Rutse Hardenberg,	
		Cornelius Van der Mulen.
Tappan,	Samuel Verbryck,	Roelif Van Houten.
Albany,	Eilardus Westerlo,	H. Gansevoort
New York,	{ Lambertus de Ronde, { Archibald Laidlie, { John H. Livingston,	{ Jacobus Van Zanten { Isaac Roosevelt. { Evert Byvanck. { Cornelius Sebring.
Aquackenong,	David Marinus.	Chr. Gerbrand Jurriaen.
Freehold and Middletown,	Benjamin Dubois,	Aart Sipkin.
Kingston,		{ Jacobus Eltinge. { Adolph Meyer.

the healing of dissensions and promotion of peace in the churches. Third, correspondence with the Church in Holland, it being provided that the minutes of the general body should be regularly sent to the classes, or if need be, the synod of North Holland might be appealed to in case of differences "on important doctrines among the brethren."

In October, 1772, the convention again assembled, and a letter from the Classis of Amsterdam, fragrant with the spirit of Christian charity, was read, in which they declared their full approbation and ratification of the plan, and expressed their earnest wishes and prayers for the prosperity of the American churches. Thus were the wounds of the bleeding Church healed and harmony was restored among her ministers and members.*

Let any one who is disposed to wonder why the first Church that was planted in New Amsterdam does not now cover the land, review the ground over which we have passed. Let him bear in mind that the Dutch rule lasted only thirty-six years after the introduction of the Church; that it departed when New Amsterdam was a little village with fifteen hundred inhabitants; that for most of the time until the establishment of national independence, the chief portion of the Church struggled for life under the shadow of a virtual Episcopal establishment; let him remember that her doors were closed to Calvinistic Presbyterians coming from Scotland and Ireland, for a century and a quarter, by the tongue unknown to them in which she spoke; and that these people began to establish churches for themselves, forty-five years before an English word was heard in a Dutch Church, and thus the opportunity of

*See this letter in Appendix to " Centennial of the Theological Seminary." p. 312.

gaining accessions from them was never enjoyed; and
that at the same time immigration from the Fatherland
ceased. Moreover, let him remember that for a century and a half she had no organized existence here,
no higher court than a consistory, and no power of
ordination; that she was simply an unorganized dependent on a foreign Church, and was at the same time
torn by internal dissensions. How could she make progress? Was she not as a bush burning but not consumed?

The Church seemed now to have arrived at a favorable position, to begin to spread and to tell on the surrounding population. But the chief thing was still
lacking, the provision for the education of her ministers; for of all the Churches in the land, she was
least able to succeed without an educated ministry, inasmuch as the people had been taught to regard that
as essential. This was required by the plan of union,
and the Church of Holland would never have consented to the independence of the American churches,
if this had not been guaranteed. In the Fatherland
great importance was attached to learning in the ministry, and no country has produced a greater proportion
of eminent theologians than Holland. The ministry
of the Dutch churches in this country was standing in
the front rank, and the fear lest that position should be
lost, powerfully urged the Conferentie to take the stand
they did. At once therefore, the subject of a professorship of theology was agitated, and measures were taken
for its establishment. "The Reformed Dutch Church
is thus entitled to the credit of having first contemplated
and adopted a system of theological education in this
country, which has received the approbation and been
followed by the practice of almost all her sister
Churches.*

*Sermon by the Rev. Thomas Dewitt, D.D., on the death of
Dr. Livingston.

In 1773, it was resolved by the general meeting of ministers and elders held at Kingston, N. Y., to ask the Classis of Amsterdam to send a Professor of Divinity from Holland. The Classis having consulted with the Theological Faculty of Utrecht agreed, instead of sending a man, to recommend the election of Dr. Livingston to the office. He would have been appointed in 1775, had not the war of the Revolution just broken out, causing the adjournment of the assembly after a day of fasting and prayer had been appointed.

The Church now had her share of trial in the troublous times that followed. Congregations were scattered, and only a small remnant of the church of New York remained in the city. The four pastors retired into the country: De Ronde to Scaghticoke, Ritzema to Kinderhook, Laidlie to Redhook, and Livingston to Kingston, N. Y., with the family of his father-in-law, Hon. Philip Livingston who was a member of Congress and a signer of the Declaration of Independence. He afterwards went to Albany, where he preached for some time, then to Livingston's Manor, where he remained eighteen months officiating every Lord's day in Dutch and English, and finally went to his father's residence in Poughkeepsie, where he remained until the close of the war.

After the city had been evacuated by the British, Dr. Livingston returned and resumed his labors with mingled emotions of joy and sadness. Of the four pastors who were there at the beginning of the war, he now stood alone. The excellent Laidlie had died, and De Ronde and Ritzema were too infirm to return. Two of the churches had been desecrated. The Middle church had been used both for a prison and a riding-school, and the North for a prison. The South church in Garden street had not been abused, and in it the scattered members of the congregation were re-collected, and there they worshiped until the other edifices had been repaired. The subject of the professorship was at once agitated, and Dr. Livingston was promptly and unanimously elected Professor of Theology in 1784. In the following year, articles of correspondence were agreed upon between the Presbyterian. Associate Reformed, and Reformed Dutch Churches.

The plan of union had answered its purpose admirably. but the time had now come for a more thorough and efficient organization of the churches. It was also thought necessary that the Standards of Doctrine, the Liturgy, and the Rules of Church Order should be published in the English language for the sake of " the general protection of the civil authorities in freedom of worship," and also because English was the national tongue, was making rapid progress, was used very extensively in the congregations, and because the " rising generation seem to be little acquainted with the Dutch tongue." After four years attention to this work by able committees, it was finished and approved in 1792. The most important part of the work was the formation of the " Explanatory Articles." which were intended to show how the Church Orders of Dort, which had been retained, were to be carried out in the new and peculiar circumstances in which the Church was placed in this country. The printed volume containing the Doctrinal Standards, Liturgy and Rules of Church Government was presented to the Synod in October 1793, was accepted and was recommended to all the congregations.

"The adoption of this Constitution," says Dr. Gunn, " is a memorable event. as it established that consolidation of the Union, without which, it was much to be feared, the Union would be but of temporary duration ;

and placed the Church in a position to maintain her character, to make herself known and respected among other denominations, and to prosecute with life and energy any enterprise, the successful accomplishment of which might be deemed essential to her future prosperity; and of the Constitution, it may be averred that it has proved the palladium (if the term be allowable) of the Church, or rather the great safeguard, next to the Bible, under the Divine blessing of her government, peace and purity. It is a good caution, "Remove not the ancient landmarks which thy fathers have set." *

Thus was the Church brought through most trying times by her Divine Head. The chief instrument that He used deserves all of the honor that we have given him, for he was a burning and shining light, and many rejoiced in his light. We will have occasion again to speak of him, for God continued him long as a counselor of the Church and a teacher of her teachers. Nor should the names of his friends and co-workers, Laidlie, Westerlo, Romeyn, Meier, Hardenberg, Leydt, Verbryck, Jackson, Rysdyck and many others be forgotten for they secured for us our goodly heritage. "Blessed are the dead which die in the Lord from henceforth; yea, saith the Spirit, that they may rest from their labors, and their works do follow them."

*Gunn's memoirs of Livingston, p. 318.

CHAPTER V.

EDUCATIONAL INSTITUTIONS, BOARDS, MISSIONS.

The history of the Church from the adoption of the Constitution to the present time is marked by the establishment and increasing efficiency of her educational institutions, her various boards, and other agencies for carrying on her work, and her progress in this country and in heathen lands.

Great importance was, as we have seen, attached in Holland to a learned ministry, and the churches in America were provided with it during the period of their dependence. The fear that this blessing might be lost was the cause of woful and almost fatal dissensions; and when the time came for the American churches to begin an independent career, it was agreed by all parties in adopting the Plan of Union that provision should at once be made for the education of candidates for the ministry. For many years the fostering of her educational institutions has been her chief object, and in the "Acts of the General Synod," the highest place has been accorded to the Professorate. Through many difficulties the Church has succeeded in making what, considering her size and strength, is a munificent provision for the education of young men for her ministry.

QUEEN'S, NOW RUTGERS COLLEGE, AND THE THEOLOGICAL SCHOOL AT NEW BRUNSWICK, N. J.

These institutions have no organic connection, the College being governed by a self-perpetuating board of trustees according to its charter, and the Seminary

directly by the General Synod according to the constitution of the Church. But their relations from the
beginning have been so intimate, that their early histories connot well be written separately. The persevering
efforts of the members of the coetus party for the
establishment of a college, to prepare men for the ministry of the Dutch Church, and to be entirely independent of other denominations, were rewarded at last by
the grant of a charter for an institution to be called
Queen's College. This charter was granted by King
George III., through Gov. William Franklin of New
Jersey, and was dated Nov. 10, 1766. It was provided
that the first meeting of the Trustees should be held at
Hackensack, N. J., on the second Tuesday in May, 1767.*
Because of certain defects in this charter, the College
never went into operation under it, and so a second
and amended charter was obtained by royal authority
through Gov. Franklin, bearing date March 20th, 1770.

The Trustees held their first meetings at Hackensack,
N. J., and the question whether the College should be
located in that village or at New Brunswick, was decided
in favor of the latter, chiefly on the ground of the larger
pecuniary inducements offered by the people of New
Brunswick. The Rev. Dr. Theodorick Romeyn having
declined the presidency, Rev. Dr. Jacobus R. Hardenbergh of Rosendale, New York, was elected in 1785, and
he was at the same time chosen pastor of the Reformed
Dutch Church of New Brunswick. He had been a
student of the Rev. John Frelinghuysen, of Raritan,
N.J.; was one of those who had been ordained by the
Coetus, a man of strong native powers; and to the reputation of an eminent divine, he added that of an ardent
and influential patriot. He was a member of the conven-

*See Centennial of New Brunswick Seminary, page 332.

tion which framed the first constitution of New Jersey. He died in 1790 at the age of fifty-two. The first tutors who gave instruction in the College were Frederick, afterwards Gen. Frelinghuysen of Revolutionary memory, the step-son of Pres. Hardenbergh; and John Taylor, who took an active part in the war of the Revolution, drilled the students as a military company, and was made Colonel of the New Jersey State regiment.

Rev. Drs. Livingston and Theodorick Romeyn having both declined the presidency after the death of Dr. Hardenbergh, degrees were conferred under the temporary presidencies of Rev. Dr. William Linn and Rev. Dr. Ira Condict until the year 1795. From that time until 1807 the exercises of the College were suspended. A union with Princeton College was proposed and discussed in the Board of Trustees but the idea was abandoned, "for it was felt that the union would be nothing less than a merging of Queen's into Nassau Hall. The Trustees preferred to hold their charter and to wait patiently for a favorable time to revive the institution."

The Trustees of the College would gladly have had the Theological professorate joined to their institution at the beginning. But as the College owed its existence to one of the parties whose dissensions had only just been healed, it was considered prudent to let the theological professorate stand independently of the literary institution; in fact this was required by the plan of union. But on account of the impoverished condition of the country immediately after the Revolution, little could be done for the support of the professor. Dr. Livingston therefore continued to hold his charge in New York City, at the same time teaching theology to his students at his home. To accommodate such as were not able to bear the expense of living in the city, Rev. Dr. Hermanus Meyer, of Pompton Plains, N. J., was appointed lector in theology, and after his death, Rev. Dr. T. Romeyn, of Schenectady, and Rev. Dr. Solomon Froeligh of Schraalenberg, were appointed lectors for the convenience of students from the northern and southern parts of the Church respectively.

The consistory of the church in New York, in order to remove the objection of expensive living in the city, now agreed that Dr. Livingston should thenceforth render them half his usual service, relinquish half his salary, and open his divinity school at Flatbush, Long Island. He removed thither in 1796, and began his lectures with a flattering number of students. But the very next year, the Synod, utterly discouraged by the difficulty of raising moneys, abandoned for the time all efforts in that direction and appointed the lectors Romeyn and Froeligh additional professors of theology. Dr. Livingston, in consequence of this virtual desertion of his school, returned to New York, and resumed full pastoral work, at the same time teaching divinity to the students who came to him.

The Synod, having learned that this plan did not work well, came back in 1804 to the original idea of one permanent endowed professorship. The election of Dr. Livingston had been made in 1784 by the Particular Synod, and he was now chosen by the General Synod to be the permanent professor, while Profs. Romeyn and Froeligh were to continue in their positions for life, but were not to have successors. It was resolved to attempt to raise funds for the support of Prof. Livingston and so to prepare the way for his separation from his pastoral charge and for his entire devotion to his professorship.

In 1807, the Trustees of Queen's College, being desirous of reviving the institution, proposed to the General Synod a union of the College and the Theological professorate, engaging to make the College subservient to the great end for which the charter had been obtained, "the promotion of a faithful and able ministry in the Dutch Church." This union was effected and it was agreed that the trustees should raise moneys for the support of the Synod's professor of theology, who should, without additional salary, serve the College as President, and also as the professor of theology, required by the charter of the College.*

In accordance with this agreement, Dr. Livingston, in the year 1810, at the age of 64, removed to New Brunswick, where he continued Professor of theology, teaching in his own house, and also as President of the College until his death in 1825. His school opened with five students: Thomas DeWitt, John S. Mabon, Robert Bronk, Peter S. Wynkoop, and a Mr. Barclay. Dr. Livingston devoted his time and strength to his professorial work, while the Rev. Dr. Condict, and after him Rev. Dr. Schureman, Vice-presidents of the College, relieved him from the cares connected with its government and discipline.

The efforts made by the trustees to increase the professorial fund met with encouraging success. It was, however, inadequate for a long time, and the deficiency was in a measure supplied by means of subscriptions and collections in the churches. The College also languished for want of funds to carry on its work, and suffered from the lack of a suitable building.

In 1809, the foundation was laid of the present main college edifice, which contained, when finished, a chapel, library, laboratory, recitation rooms, and also two res-

*All the Covenants made at various times by the General Synod and the Trustees of the College, have been published in the "Centennial of the Theol. Seminary," p. 363.

idences for professors. In 1816 the exercises of the College were suspended until 1825.

In the theological school Dr. Livingston continued to be sole professor until 1815, aided, however, by teachers of Hebrew, first Rev. Dr. Bassett and afterwards Rev. Dr. Jeremiah Romeyn, and Rev. Dr. John M. Van Harlingen, who were pastors of churches and taught students in their parsonages.

In 1815, Rev. John Schureman, D.D., Vice-president of the College and pastor of the Dutch Church in New Brunswick, was elected Professor of Pastoral Theology and Ecclesiastical History. The churches of Albany and New Brunswick made liberal contributions to his salary and vigorous efforts were made to meet deficiencies by annual collections in the churches. In two and a half years the Church was called to mourn over his removal by death.

Rev. Thomas DeWitt having declined to fill the vacancy, Rev. John S. Mabon and Rev. James S. Cannon were temporarily engaged to give instruction in these branches of study.

In 1819, Rev. John Ludlow was appointed Professor of Biblical Literature and Ecclesiastical History, and continued in this office until 1823, when he removed to the North Dutch Church in the city of Albany, and his place was filled by the Rev. John DeWitt D.D., of the South Dutch Church of Albany.

It was just at this time that Dr. Livingston called upon and urged the churches to arise and make a united, determined and persistent effort for a more full endowment of the theological school, so that a corps of three professors might be supported, and to his appeal he added a liberal subscription. The history of this noble work we cannot here give nor even mention the names of those who zealously carried it to a successful issue.

The enthusiasm was universal and the liberality of both ministers and laymen was remarkable. In a short time over $25,000 were raised in the Particular Synod of New York for a second professorship, and the same amount in the Particular Synod of Albany for a third.*

Before the effort was finished, but not until its success had been assured, the venerable and beloved Livingston was called away and entered into his rest. His death took place Jan. 20th, 1825. He had served the Church fifty-five years as a minister and forty-one as a professor of theology. While lecturing to his students on the day before his death, on the subject of Divine Providence, he alluded to the Saviour's dying exclamation, " It is finished " and added, " His work was done, and then His Father took him home, and just so He will do with me ; when my work is done, my Father will take me home." In usual health, he retired to rest. In the morning his little grandson called him but received no answer. The spirit had departed, and the body was lying on the bed in an easy posture, indicating that the separation had taken place without a struggle. It is well known that he had always been troubled not with the fear of death, but of the pains of dying, and it was his constant prayer that he might never experience them. Was not that prayer granted ?

Dr. Livingston, it will readily be seen, was an extraordinary man, a man of learning, wisdom and piety, raised up by God and qualified to meet the wants of the times. His students in their old age loved to bring up pleasant reminiscences of their intercourse with him in his lecture-room, and in his home. His personal appearance was commanding, and his manners those of a perfect gentleman of the old school ; he was at home in the

*Centennial of the Theol. Seminary p. 194.

theological room, and in the pulpit he spoke with uncommon power. Never should the Reformed Dutch Church forget its "debt of gratitude to this man of God who, from the time that he entered the ministry was, for more than half a century, the guiding and directing mind of the Church in every important work. He was not only the father of our system of theological education and the first professor, but he was the eloquent advocate of missions ; he shaped our constitutional law, and adapted the psalmody for church worship, and put the impress of his mind not only on the ministry but the whole Church." *

Rev. Philip Milledoler, D.D., one of the pastors of the Collegiate Church in New York, was inaugurated as the successor of Dr. Livingston May 25, 1825, in the chair of Didactic and Polemic Theology. Rev. Selah S. Woodhull, D.D., Pastor of the Ref. Dutch Church of Brooklyn, was elected Professor of Ecclesiastical History, Church Government, and Pastoral Theology and was inaugurated on the second Wednesday of November, 1825. Thus at the close of the year 1825, there were three professors in active service in the theological school.

In the year 1825 Queen's College was revived and took the name of Rutgers, in honor of Col. Henry Rutgers, of New York City, a liberal contributor to its funds. The fact that the theological school now had a corps of three professors who might be induced to teach in the College without additional salary, suggested the idea of this revival of the College. It is claimed, and probably on good grounds, that the suggestion came from the professors of theology themselves. At any rate they heartily entered into the arrangement which was agreed upon

* Centennial of the Theol. Seminary, p 101.

by the Trustees and the General Synod. In September, 1825 the Synod and Trustees made a covenant by which the Synod engaged that the professors of theology should do service in the College, and that the College should have the free use of the building which had, by purchase become the property of the Synod. The Trustees engaged to appoint and support a professor of languages and also one of mathematics, and to elect one of the professors of theology President of the College. Under this covenant, the professors of theology did a large part of the work in the College for many years, and it is beyond question that the College could not have been in any other way resuscitated at that time. They were gradually relieved as the College became able to increase its corps of professors.

With the resignation of President Milledoler in 1840, the agreement that one of the professors of theology should be elected President of the College was annulled, and the Hon. A. Bruyn Hasbrouck, LL.D., of Kingston, N. Y., was chosen to that office. He resigned in 1850 and Hon. Theodore Frelinghuysen, LL.D., at that time Chancellor of the University of the City of New York, and before that U. S. Senator from New Jersey, was chosen to fill the vacancy.

President Frelinghuysen was removed by death in 1862 and Rev. William H. Campbell, D.D., LL.D., who had for thirteen years been professor of Biblical Literature in the Theological Seminary, was elected in his stead. Under his presidency a very successful effort for the increase of the endowment was made and the Rutgers Scientific School, embracing the State Agricultural College, was established, and the course of instruction was widely extended.

President Campbell having resigned in 1881, Merrill Edwards Gates, Ph.D., LL.D. L.H.D., principal of the

Albany Academy was elected President of the College. A full corps of professors is associated with him in the classical and scientific departments.

A preparatory Grammar School is connected with the College and is under the care of the Trustees who appoint the head-master and supervise the work of the school.

The President of the College is required by its charter to be a member in full communion of the Reformed Church in America, and by covenant between the Trustees and the General Synod made in 1864, three-fourths of the Trustees also, must be members in full communion of said Church. The College therefore has a fair claim on the members of this denomination for support and patronage. Moreover it is prepared to do all the work of a college well, and so to perform its allotted part in the work of preparing young men for the ministry of the Reformed Church in accordance with the purpose of its charter. This work it has done nobly, and without intermission from the time of its revival in 1825 under the name of Rutgers.

The arrangement of 1825 between the Trustees and Synod had scarcely been made when both institutions and the whole Church were called to mourn the loss of Prof. Woodhull, who departed this life Feb. 27th, 1826, only three months after his induction into office.

Rev. James S. Cannon, D.D., pastor of the Reformed Dutch Church of Six Mile Run, N. J., was appointed successor to Prof. Woodhull and was inaugurated on the first Wednesday in May, 1826.

Rev. Prof. John Dewitt, D. D. was removed by death Oct. 11th 1831. He died in the prime of life being only forty-two years of age. His successor was the Rev. Alexander McClelland, D.D., Prof. of Languages in Rutgers College, who was inaugurated July 19th, 1832.

The year 1835 was marked by the completion of an effort for increasing the permanent fund which resulted in the addition of $ 34,050 to it.

The discouragement caused by the fewness of the students was now removed by the result of the great revival of 1836-7. In the autumn of 1837, a class of fifteen was received, which was the largest thus far that had ever been admitted to the school. The Theological school not only, but the Church at large continued to reap the blessed fruits of that revival for many years.

In the year 1841, Prof. Milledoler resigned his professorship in the Seminary, and the Rev. Samuel A. Van Vranken, D.D., Pastor of the Reformed Dutch Church in Broome St., New York, was inaugurated as his successor on the 2nd Tuesday in December, 1841.

Prof. McClelland, after twenty years of faithful and exceptionally able service, was compelled on account of the state of his health, to offer his resignation, which was reluctantly accepted by the Synod in June, 1851. He died in New Brunswick in 1864. The same Synod that accepted his resignation chose as his successor the Rev. William H. Campbell, D.D., LL.D., at the time principal of the Albany Academy. He remained in this office working with untiring energy for the interests of the institution until June 1863, when he retired to take the Presidency of Rutgers College which had been made vacant by the death of the Hon. Theodore Frelinghuysen, LL.D.

In June, 1852, Prof. Cannon being disabled by disease sent in his resignation to the General Synod, which declared him Professor Emeritus. In less than two months he was removed by death. Rev. John Ludlow, D.D., LL.D., Provost of the University of Pennsylvania was elected his successor and was inaugurated Oct. 1st, 1852.

Profs. Van Vranken, Campbell and Ludlow constituted the Theological Faculty at this time, and by them a movement was made for procuring a commodious building for the uses of the institution. The result was the erection of the Peter Hertzog Theological Hall which was dedicated and opened on the 23rd of September, 1856.

For its erection, Mrs. Anna Hertzog, a member of the Third Reformed Dutch Church of Philadelphia gave § 30,700 and named the building in honor of her deceased husband. She subsequently left a legacy of $10,000 to the General Synod, the interest of which must be used to keep the building in repair.* It contains studies and dormitories for the students, a chapel, reading-room, dining-room, and formerly the library, lecture-rooms and museum were also contained in it. It is lighted by gas, and provided with water from the city works, and students preparing for the ministry find in it a comfortable home. Until the time of the opening of this Hall, the books belonging to the College and Seminary had formed one library which was deposited in the College building; but now a division was made and the books belonging to the latter were removed to the new Hall. They have since been deposited in the Gardner A. Sage Library. The additional buildings that have been erected on the campus are the James Suydam Hall, the gift of James Suydam, Esq., containing gymnasium, lecture-rooms, museum, and chapel; the fire-proof Gardner A. Sage Library, the gift of Gardner A. Sage, Esq.; and four professorial residences, one of which was built with money bequeathed by Mr. James Suydam for the object. A fifth professorial residence the gift of Messrs. Suydam and Sage is on the corner of Seminary Place and George streets, outside of the campus. The chief portion of the

*See note on Mrs. Hertzog in Corwin's Manual, (1879,) p. 109.

spacious campus, in the center of which Peter Hertzog Theological Hall stands on a beautiful and commanding site, was the liberal gift of Col. James Neilson, of New Brunswick; additional lots were given by Messrs. David Bishop and Charles P. Dayton of the same city; and to make a complete rectangle, additional ground was bought with $2,000 contributed by Messrs. Francis and Wessell Wessells, of Paramus, N. J. The property has been placed by the General Synod in charge of a standing committee composed of six persons, one of whom is a member of the Faculty, and which reports annually to the General Synod.

On the 8th of September, 1857, Prof. Ludlow departed this life, and Rev. Samuel M. Woodbridge, D.D., Pastor of the Second Reformed Dutch Church of New Brunswick was chosen his successor and was inaugurated Dec. 2, 1857.

The death of Prof. Van Vranken took place Jan. 1, 1861, and on the 24th of September of the same year, Rev. Joseph F. Berg, D.D., Pastor of the Second Ref. Dutch Church of Philadelphia, was inaugurated his successor.

Prof. Campbell having resigned in 1863, Rev. John Dewitt, D.D., Pastor of the Reformed Dutch Church of Millstone, N. J., was elected his successor and was inaugurated Sept. 22, 1863. In the following year, 1864, the College property was by the General Synod reconveyed to the Trustees of the College and the next year the Synod relinquished their covenant right to nominate the Professor of Divinity in the College, required by the charter.

From this period we date the beginning of movements and of gifts having in view an increased efficiency of the Theological School. The first was the establishment of **the Professorship of Pastoral Theology and Sacred**

Rhetoric, to which the Rev. David D. Demarest, D.D., Pastor of the Reformed Dutch Church of Hudson, N. Y., was elected, and who was inaugurated Sept. 19th, 1865. The moneys for the endowment of this professorship were contributed by the churches under the stimulus of the conditional offer by an individual of $ 40.000 to be added to the existing Professorial Fund. The unhappy failure to receive that which had in good faith and with the noblest purpose been promised, providentially opened the way for the munificent benefactions since received from many liberal friends, through the instrumentality of the Rev. James A. H. Cornell, D.D., who gave himself wholly to work for the Seminary during two and a half years. The plan of this volume forbids us to enter into the interesting details, but the grand results should awaken heartfelt thanks to God, and secure for the donors and agent the everlasting remembrance of the Church.

Exceedingly prominent among these donors were James Suydam, Esq., and Gardner A. Sage, Esq., of New York City, who not only gave largely while Dr. Cornell was at work, but continued to counsel with him, and largely through his influence they by will left legacies to the institution.* Thus has the James Suydam Professorship of Didactic and Polemic Theology been endowed, and a dwelling provided for the professor; also, the Gardner A. Sage Professorship of New Testament Exegesis and a dwelling for the professor; the James Suydam Hall containing lecture-rooms, gymnasium, chapel and museum; the Gardner A. Sage fire-proof Library; funds invested, the income of which is used for keeping buildings in repair and grounds in order; for the main-

---

* For Biographical notices of Messrs. Suydam and Sage, and an account of their gifts to the Seminary, see " Centennial of the Theol, Seminary," pp. 136, 390.

tenance of Peter Hertzog Hall; for the contingent
expenses of Suydam Hall; for the salary of the Libra-
rian, and all contigent expenses of the Library, and for
the purchase of books: also a number of scholarships
for the benefit of needy students. The aggregate of the
donations of these two men amount to a half million of
dollars, nearly equally divided between them. Many
other noble men and women did liberal things for the
increase of the endowment and especially for the
increase of the Library, a number giving $2.500 each so
that $55.000 were available for the purchase of books
additional to the old Library which had already been
enriched by the gift of 3,500 volumes by Mrs. Mary
Bethune from the library of her lamented husband Rev.
George W. Bethune, D.D. This Library now contains
over 40,000 well-selected volumes, and is second in value
to none in the country as a working theological library.
New works in every department are added as they
appear.*

The Vedder Lecture on the " Present Aspects of Modern Infidelity including its Cause and Cure," to be delivered before both College and Seminary, was established
in 1873 by Nicholas T. Vedder, of Utica N. Y., by the
gift of $10,000 in rail-road securities. After two
courses had been delivered, the payment of interest on
the bonds which the Synod, by direction of the donor
was to hold until the principal should become due,
ceased. Consequently all the subsequent lecturers have
done their work without pecuniary compensation. The
Synod of 1888 resolved that lecturers should not be
appointed thereafter.

The death of Prof. Berg took place July 20th, 1871.

*For full details of the work of Dr. Cornell in enlarging
the endowments and securing funds for the various needs of
the Seminary, see " Centennial of the Seminary " 1884.

and Prof. Woodbridge filled the vacancy for one year, when Rev. Abraham B. Van Zandt, D.D., Pastor of the Ref. Church of Montgomery, N. Y., was elected, and was inaugurated Sept. 24, 1872. After nine years of service, being disabled by a long and painful illness, Prof. Van Zandt offered his resignation to the General Synod in June 1881; it was accepted, and on the 21st of July following he died. His successor, Rev. William V. V. Mabon, D.D., Pastor of the Reformed Church of New Durham, N. J., was inaugurated Dec. 5th, 1881.

In 1871 the Centennial Anniversary of the Convention of ministers and elders to form the " Plan of Union ", was observed; and in 1876, the Centennial Anniversary of National Independence was celebrated by a series of sermons on various phases of the history and characteristics of the Church, delivered by prominent ministers of the denomination. These able discourses have been published in a volume of permanent value, called " Centennial Discourses."

In June, 1884, the Rev. John G. Lansing, Pastor of the Reformed Church of West Troy, was elected to the newly established Gardner A. Sage Professorship of Old Testament Exegesis and Literature, and was inaugurated Sept. 23rd, 1884.

The same year was marked by the memorable Centennial Anniversary of the election of Rev. John H. Livingston, D.D., as the first Professor of Theology in the Reformed Dutch Church in America. The surpassing interest of this occasion can never be forgotten by those who were present. A historical, and various other addresses were delivered; many theological seminaries were represented, and presented their congratulations, as did also Rutgers and Hope Colleges. The review of the dealings of God with the institution during the century of its existence, awakened devout thankfulness, and holy faith and courage. In the memorial volume of the proceedings, every lover of the Reformed Dutch Church will find a mine of information, not only concerning the Theological Seminary and Rutgers College, but in many matters of interest connected with the history of the denomination. About 900 students have thus far been connected with this theological school.

UNION COLLEGE AT SCHENECTADY, N. Y.

Union College was not founded as was Queen's, for the express purpose of aiding in the preparation of students for the ministry in the Reformed Dutch Church; nor was it ever brought into such covenant relations with the General Synod and the theological school as Queen's (Rutgers) held for many years. Yet it is entitled to notice in this connection, because it arose out of the Schenectady Academy, which was founded in 1785, by the Rev. Theodorick Romeyn, D.D., Pastor of the Reformed Dutch Church in Schenectady, and which, converted into a College, was chartered by the Legislature of New York in 1795. Dr. Romeyn was at that time a lector in Theology, and in 1797 he was made Professor of Theology by the General Synod. But this College is more especially worthy of mention, because it was for many years the principal feeder of the Theological School at New Brunswick. Many will be surprised to learn, that of the students connected with our Seminary previously to the year 1834, fifty-seven were graduates of Union College and thirty-seven of Queen's (Rutgers). The long continued suspension of the exercises in the College at New Brunswick doubtless had much to do with this, and perhaps also something is to be attributed to long-lingering prejudices arising out of the Coetus and Conferentie controversy.

Since 1834, Rutgers has been the principal source of supply to the Seminary, having furnished it with far more students than have come from all other colleges. Two of the present Professors of Theology, who were graduated from the Theological School at New Brunswick, are alumni of Union College. And of those who have at different times served in the ministry of the Reformed Dutch Church, about 130 were graduated from Union College.*

HOPE COLLEGE AND THE WESTERN THEOLOGICAL SEMINARY AT HOLLAND, MICH.

Besides these ancient institutions are those of later origin, Hope College and the Western Theological Seminary established at Holland, Mich., and the Northwestern Academy at Orange City, Iowa, to meet the wants of the churches in the western part of our country. These owe their origin to the emigrants from the Netherlands, who, leaving their Fatherland for the sake of Gospel liberty, came under the lead of Rev. Albertus C. Van Raalte, D.D., in 1846-7, and settled in the western part of Michigan on Black Lake. One of their first concerns was to have an institution of learning in which their children might be educated with a view to the holy ministry. Before this, as early as 1843, the subject of education in the west had been brought to the notice of the General Synod, and the report on the state of the Church presented by Rev. James Romeyn to the General Synod in 1848, treated it quite fully. The Rev. Dr. Van Raalte established a school very soon after the arrival of the first colonists, known as the Holland Academy, which was aided by the Board

---

*See sketch of Union College in its relations to the Reformed Church in Corwin's Manual, (1879,) p. 116; also Schenectady First Church Memorial.

of Domestic Missions, and was subsequently placed
under the care of the Board of Education, and which
had a succession of able principals, until 1863 when the
General Synod resolved that it should be converted
into a college. A board of Superintendents, and Professors were appointed and measures were taken for
obtaining an endowment. The institution received its
charter as Hope College in 1866, just one century
after Queen's College had received its first charter, and
the Rev. Philip Phelps, Jr., D. D., was chosen its President. The first class was graduated the same year, and
the members of it who had the ministry in view were
permitted by the Synod to pursue preparatory theological studies there under the direction of the President and professors of the College.

In 1867, the Rev. Cornelius E. Crispell, D.D., was
elected Professor of Didactic and Polemic Theology;
the students of theology were placed under his care,
and he was assisted by the President of the College,
and the Professors Beck, Oggel, and Scott, whom the
Synod had authorized to act as lectors in the several
branches which they had taught the preceding year.
The Council of Hope College was made the Board of
Superintendents of the theological department. In
1877, the General Synod resolved "that, in view of the
present embarrassed condition of the finances of the
College, the Council be directed for the present to sus-
pend the theological department." The resignation
of Prof. Crispell was accepted by the Synod in 1879.
Efforts which had been made during this period to procure moneys for the endowment, and which had not
been very successful, were after a season, resumed; and
the Synod of 1884 resolved to restore the teaching of
Theology as soon as moneys paid in for the endowment
should reach the sum of $30,000. It elected Rev. Nich-

olas M. Steffens, D.D., Professor of Didactic and Polemic Theology with the condition that his inauguration should take place when the above sum should have been placed in the hands of the Board of Direction, and $700 per year should have been secured for the services of a lector. The Professor was accordingly inaugurated December 4th, 1884. Rev. Henry N. Dosker was appointed Lector, and classes for the study of theology were again formed. By the General Synod of 1888, the Rev. John W. Beardslee, D.D., was elected Professor of Biblical Languages, Literature and Exegesis. From this school 37 students have thus far received professorial certificates. In 1885, the Rev. Charles Scott, D.D., who had for some time acted as provisional President of Hope College, was elected successor of Rev. Dr. Phelps in the office of President.

NORTHWESTERN CLASSICAL ACADEMY, ORANGE CITY, IA.

This institution is in the sixth year of its existence and is going forward hopefully and prosperously under the care of its Principal, Rev. J. A. de Spelder. This young institution, situated on the frontier, has a special claim to the fostering care of the Church, because of its bearing on the missionary work in the Far West. The General Synod at its last session, 1888, reiterated its former declarations that this growing academy merits the full confidence of the Church; and endorsed the efforts of its governing board to secure its endowment, and also recommended it to the Board of Education for aid.

THE BOARD OF EDUCATION.

The cases of worthy, indigent young men desiring the ministry received consideration as soon as efforts for the establishment of a theological school were commenced, and it was at once resolved that such young men should be aided from the funds raised for the Professorate. Collections for this purpose were made in the churches, and the Trustees of Queen's College and the members of the General Synod were of one mind on this subject. A great and lasting impulse was given to the cause of beneficiary education, when the Rev. Elias Van Bunschooten gave, in 1814, the sum, munificent for the times, of $14,640 which was by his will increased to $18,000, the income of which was to be used in aiding indigent students preparing for the ministry. These moneys were allowed to accumulate until the sum of $20,000 was reached, when distribution of the income began to be made. For more than 70 years has this Fund been doing its beneficent work, and it continues still to do it. The large numbers of those who have done nobly in the establishment of scholarships have followed the example of this first generous benefactor, whose name is worthy of being held in grateful remembrance by so many of our ministers.

In 1828, an Educational Society was formed by individual ministers and members of the Church, which gave place in 1832 to the Board of Education, established by the General Synod, to which it transferred its funds. This Board receives money by collections in the churches, which, in the year ending May, 1888, amounted to $8,476.18. In addition, there is an income from a number of scholarships of which, some are held by the General Synod, and some by the Board of Education. There are also some funds held by the Trustees of Rutgers College, given by the donors for the same purpose, and the income of which is disbursed by the trustees. A very large proportion of the ministers of our Church have been aided from these various sources.

It is safe to say that this cause is second in importance to none now before the Church, and is one that should excite an ever-deepening interest. When we consider that the number of candidates for the ministry must increase; that we constantly pray for their increase; that the proportion of those needing aid is likely to be as great in the future as it is in the present, and that our educational institutions in the West demand the fostering care of the Church; it seems clear that we should spend much more for those objects per annum than $22.000, which was the amount disbursed in the year 1888, and that the receipts from the churches should be very largely increased.

Young men, in order to receive aid from the Board, must be recommended by consistories to classes; and are received with the understanding that they are to pursue and complete their theological studies in institutions that are under the care of the General Synod.

THE BOARD OF SABBATH SCHOOL UNION.

In the year 1839, the Board of Sabbath School Union was formed, the object of which was to increase an interest in Sunday Schools and to secure, as far as possible, the teaching of the catechisms of the Church in them. The power of this Board was advisory, acting in concert with pastors and consistories, and so doing an excellent work in the revival of catechetical instruction. It published some useful volumes for the young, established new schools, and aided and encouraged feeble ones. This Board was abolished by the General Synod in 1862, and so much of its business as related to missionary operations, was placed under the control of the Board of Domestic Missions, and so much as related to publications was placed in charge of the Board of Publication.

THE BOARD OF PUBLICATION.

The Board of Publication was formed in the year 1854, by the General Synod, "for the publication and the circulation of all the the religious works which are designed for general diffusion among the churches under its care," and it made it the duty of the executive committee to "select and prepare suitable tracts and books for publication, to superintend and direct their distribution. etc." This Board has, in its field done, and is doing good work for the denomination as well as for our common Christianity. For some years it published the "Sower and Mission Monthly," which has now been superseded by the "Mission Field," a magazine, published by this, in connection with the other Boards. In its last report, 1888, it is said: "It must not be forgotten that donations to weak churches and to Christian work in various fields, or selling books and tracts at cost, or little above it, is the very purpose for which the Board of Publication was created and exists. Its object calls for and its sound management deserves the substantial sympathy and free-hearted liberality of the churches."

THE WIDOWS' FUND.

By one of the rules of Church Government established by the Synod of Dort (13), it was required that provision should be made "for the widows and orphans of ministers in general." Such provision was expressly guaranteed in some of the calls of the first ministers who came to this country. Immediately after the adoption of the Articles of Union in 1771, the matter was agitated, and a plan for this purpose was drawn up, which was approved, but the War of the Revolution prevented further proceedings. The subject was again taken up after the Revolution and the matter was agitated at different times until the year 1837, when a plan was adopted, and at once carried into practical operation. After a time, serious defects in the plan became apparent, and in the year 1864, through withdrawals of money that had been paid in, nothing was left for the annuitants. It was then revised, and modified in several particulars and relieved from most of its objectionable features, and the number of subscribers has since that time been considerably increased. It has now a capital fund of $73,970.99.

Any minister of the Church may be a member by the payment of $20 per annum, or if he prefer he may pay $500 at once and be relieved from all further payments. Five or more annual payments of $20 entitle to the maximum annuity of $200, when the income of the fund will allow it. Payment for a less term than five years entitles to proportionate benefit. The superannuated or disabled minister may receive the annuity, and in case of a minister's death, the widow and the children to a certain age, are entitled to receive the amount authorized by the rules.

THE DISABLED MINISTERS' FUND.

The Disabled Ministers' Fund, formerly called the Sustentation Fund, was established in 1855, for the aid of disabled ministers, and of the families of deceased ones who may be in need. The moneys disbursed are obtained from collections in the churches and from the income of a capital sum invested amounting to $53,817.28 of which $30,000 was received as a legacy from James Suydam, Esq. A recommendation for a certain sum, must be made by the classis of which the minister is, or was a member.

DOMESTIC MISSIONS.

The Reformed Dutch Church has often been charged with being particularly slow, and far behind other denominations in Domestic Missionary work, and it is true that she has not spread over all parts of the Union, nor planted churches in every State and Territory. It was a long time before missionary work could be done at all beyond the original Dutch settlements, because of the insuperable barrier of the Dutch language; and when it was removed, means, and especially men were wanting. But the record of true missionary work performed by the earliest ministers and churches is a noble one. Down to the beginning of the present century, the Dutch churches in this country greatly outnumbered the ministers. Then, many vacant churches were cared for, some of them year after year by the settled pastors, who frequently made long and perilous journeys to visit them in order to preach to them, to catechise the children, and to administer Holy Baptism and the Lord's Supper. The congregations of these pastors cheerfully consented to their protracted absences on these missions, considering this sacrifice as their contribution to the spiritual welfare of their less-favored brethren; and they enjoyed their worship conducted by the voorlesers, while their pastors were ministering to the scattered flocks, some of whom were far distant on the edge of the wilderness. It was also expressly provided in some of the calls, that means should be used for the conversion of the Indians, not a few of whom were brought into the communion of the churches. This unorganized but truly missionary work was continued for years, and has never been duly appreciated.

The early Synods, from 1786, made church supply and church extension important matters for consideration in all their meetings. The field, of course, was confined to places where the Dutch language prevailed, but these afforded ample missionary ground for the time. Synodical action was induced by a request from the people of Saratoga, that they might be furnished with the preaching of the Word. Collections then began to be made in the churches to defray the expenses of ministers and candidates in journeying to destitute places to administer the sacraments and to organize churches. Every classis was directed to look after needy fields within its bounds, and Church Extension became an item in the regular business of every session. Appeals for ministers came from Dutch settlements in Western Virginia, in Adams Co., Pa., in Mercer Co., Ky., and from colonies in western New York. Young men, when licensed, were frequently sent on missionary tours for several months. The Classis of Albany was specially prominent and active in the work of church extension. In 1798 this Classis sent Rev. Robert Mc. Dowell as their missionary to Canada, who organized a number of churches along the St. Lawrence, and on the northern shores of Lake Ontario. The number of churches in the states of New York and New Jersey was also considerably increased. During this period ending in 1806, there was a great deal of zeal for church extension, but little of men or means, and the distant fields of Virginia and Kentucky that had been occupied, were ere long abandoned. The Conewago church in Adams Co., Pa., was broken up by the removal of the people composing it, some to Kentucky and some to western New York.

In 1806 the General Synod appointed a standing committee on missions, to be located in Albany, and to have charge of all the missionary operations of the Church. Their efforts were chiefly directed to Canada, where

Mr. McDowell continued to labor, and where there were eleven organized churches. Ministers and candidates were sent to make tours among these churches. But the Church became disheartened because of the distance and comparatively unpromising character of this field, and felt that men and means could be employed to greater advantage nearer home in the new towns and settlements. The committee was transferred to New York, and the Canadian field was quietly abandoned in 1819. In 1822, the "New York Missionary Society of the Reformed Dutch Church" was formed. It was a voluntary organization, but the Synod made its Board of Managers its own Standing Committee on Missions and urged the churches to form societies auxiliary to it.

This society entered vigorously upon its work, and gave a fresh impulse to the cause; did much in strengthening feeble churches, and in establishing new ones. It aimed to procure regular contributions from every church, and it employed the graduates from the Theological Seminary in Missionary work. Under its auspices the "Monthly Magazine of the Reformed Dutch Church" was begun in 1826, which four years afterward, was succeeded by the Christian Intelligencer.

The Particular Synod of Albany, feeling, after a time, that destitute places within its bounds were not receiving a due share of attention, the General Synod in 1828, directed the Missionary Society to appoint a northern Board to act under them. But difficulties arose from the fact, that this northern Board was nothing more than a sub-committee of the New York Missionary Society, which society was not amenable to the General Synod, and that there was a wide-spread and strong feeling that the General Synod ought to have full authority over all the missionary operations of the Church, and so the General Synod established its Board of Domestic Missions in 1831.

The Rev. John F. Schermerhorn was appointed general agent, and labored successfully for two years, organizing a number of churches in western New York. Various agents were employed until the year 1849, when the Board was reorganized, and the Rev. John Garretson, D.D., was appointed secretary, which office he held until the year 1859, and which is now held by Rev. Charles H. Pool.

In 1836, the establishment of churches in the western states began to be considered, and a commission was appointed to survey the field. The first church organized in these states was that of Fairview, Ill. where a colony of members of the Reformed Dutch Church from Somerset Co., New Jersey, chiefly from the church of Six Mile Run had settled. Soon after, others were formed in the states of Michigan, Indiana, Illinois and Wisconsin. The Holland immigration, which began under the lead of the Rev. A. C. Van Raalte D.D., in 1846, immediately added a considerable number of churches, using the Holland language, which were formed into the Classis of Holland. The immigration has continued to the present time, and churches have been established farther West, even in Kansas, Nebraska and in Dakota, where a classis was formed in the year 1888. From the report of the year 1888, we learn that 102 missionary pastors have received, during the year, from the Board for salaries $27,359.14. A very valuable auxiliary is found in the Woman's Executive Committee of Domestic Missions, which disbursed during the year $8,608.44. The specific work of this committee is that of building and repairing parsonages, sending out boxes of clothing, papers, and articles for family use. Many a parsonage has been made glad by the thoughtful ministrations of these zealous and efficient women.

In connection with the Board of Domestic Missions, is the Church Building Fund, which aids feeble churches in building houses of worship. The total income of this fund for the last year was $ 19,584.42. Money is loaned from this fund without interest to churches needing it, for the erection of houses of worship.

FOREIGN MISSIONS.

Wherever the Dutch people planted colonies in the East Indies they sent ministers of religion, and so, when settlements were made in America, ministers were sent to them. It was stipulated in the calls of some of these, that they should labor for the conversion of the surrounding heathen. This was done, to some extent, in New Jersey, and to a larger extent in New York; and we have recorded results of the work done at Albany, Schenectady, and Schoharie. The names of many Indian converts are found on the Baptismal registers of these churches. The good work was continued by Dellius and Lydius, successors of Megapolensis at Albany and also by Rev. B. Freeman at Schenectady.

The New York Missionary Society was formed in 1796, in the membership of which the Presbyterian, Baptist and Reformed Dutch denominations were represented. Dr Livingston was its Vice-president, and he preached before it two sermons of great power, one of which from the text Rev. 14 : 6, "And I saw another angel fly in the midst of heaven" etc., had great influence in promoting a missionary spirit through the country at that early day. It was republished by Samuel J. Mills, while a student in Williams College, and "was the great means of kindling the missionary spirit in that institution," which resulted in the consecration of Mills, and several other students, to the work of Foreign Missions.* It is also worthy of notice that this society established a monthly concert of prayer to be held in turn in the churches of the denominations represented in its membership.

The Northern Missionary Society representing the same denominations was formed at Albany in 1797. Of this the Rev. Theodoric Romeyn, D.D. was the first President. Its work was chiefly among the Indians of Central and Western New York, and it continued in existence until the year 1830.

In 1816, the General Assembly of the Presbyterian Church, the General Synod of the Associate Reformed Church, and the General Synod of the Reformed Dutch Church co-operated in the formation of the United Foreign Missionary Society, whose field of operation also was the American Indians. This Society continued until 1826, when it was merged into the American Board of Commissioners for Foreign Missions. The state of things that resulted soon caused dissatisfaction. It was felt that the contributions of the churches to the treasury of the American Board went virtually for the establishment of congregational churches, although the Board never required the native converts to organize themselves according to any particular form of Church government. It was therefore arranged in 1832, that ministers of our Church should be sent out by the American Board; that they should be placed in missions by themselves; that the churches gathered by them might be of our own order; that our contributions should be paid into the treasury of the American Board; and that said Board would supplement what was needed, if anything, for the support of our missions.

In due time, the feeling became strong and wide-

*See letter of Rev. J. F. Schermerhorn in the Christian Intelligencer of Oct. 6th, 1838.

spread that while this method had its advantages and was agreeable to all parties, yet, under it, the resources of the Church were not adequately called out, nor was she receiving the best missionary education, while in this state of dependence; and that it would be better for herself as well as for the cause, if she should carry on her work in the foreign field independently of the American Board. Accordingly, a separation was effected, in the most pleasant manner, in the year 1857, when the Amoy and Arcot Missions were transferred to our Board. The contributions of the Reformed Church have, since that time, increased seven or eight fold.

In 1819, John Scudder, M.D., a member of the Reformed Dutch Church in Franklin Street, New York, had gone, under the auspices of the American Board as a missionary, to Ceylon, where he was ordained in 1821, by a Council of missionaries belonging to several denominations. Thence he was transferred to Madras. He presided at the formation of the Classis of Arcot, and in 1855, he died at Wynberg in South Africa, whither he had gone to recruit. The work begun by him in India has been carried on, to a great extent, by his sons and grandsons. Rev. David Abeel went in 1829 to China, as chaplain of the American Seamen's Friend Society and he afterwards labored as a missionary in that Empire. Cornelius V. A. Van Dyck, M.D., a member of the Dutch Church of Kinderhook, went, in 1839 under the auspices of the American Board to Syria, where he was ordained by a Council of missionaries, and he is still in the service at Beyrout. Soon after the formation of our Foreign Board, a missionary spirit was awakened in the Theological School at New Brunswick, and a number of the young men declared their wish to go to the heathen. The attention of the Board was directed to Netherlands' India as containing an inviting field for their occupation.

In 1836, Rev. Messrs. Elbert Nevius, Jacob Ennis, William Youngblood and Elihu Doty with their wives, and Miss Azubah C. Condict, sister of Mrs. Nevius, embarked for Java, and they were followed, in 1838, by the Rev. Messrs. Frederick B. Thomson and William J. Pohlman and their wives. The Dutch government would allow them to settle only on the island of Borneo, and required in every case a preliminary residence of one year at Batavia. Two stations were established in Borneo, one at Pontianak on the sea coast, and one at Karangan, among the Dyaks of the interior.

Messrs. Doty and Pohlman devoted themselves to the study of the Chinese language, and in 1844 joined Mr. Abeel at Amoy, and thus the mission at Amoy, which has been so successful to the present day, was established. Meanwhile, the Rev. Messrs. Youngblood and Thomson and the Rev. Wm. H. Steele, who had gone out in 1842 to join them, labored among the Dyaks at Karangan until the two former were compelled to leave. Mr. Steele remained alone at this station until worn down by labors, and having waited in vain for reinforcements, he was directed by the Prudential Committee in 1849, to return home. The state of his health has prevented his return to the field and Karangan has been abandoned.

The Japan Mission was established in 1859, when two missionaries, Rev. Dr. S. R. Brown and Rev. Guido F. Verbeck and their wives were sent out. The intensely interesting and well known history of this mission we can only allude to. Large numbers have been converted, many churches organized, native pastors ordained, schools for boys and girls established, and in connection with Presbyterian missionaries, our missionaries teach in a theological department at Tokio. The work in Japan is wonderful, and it is full of promise for the future.

The entire number of ordained foreign missionaries connected with all our stations is 25, and of unordained 3 ; of married ladies there are 21, of unmarried 9, making a total of 58 at the present time. Our missionaries in India, China and Japan have done their full share in the work of translating the Scriptures, and of providing the people with a Christian literature in their own tongues. In 1875, the Woman's Board of Foreign Missions was established with a view of increasing the interest of the women in Foreign Missions, and especially to secure their aid in working in connection with missionaries for the welfare of women among the heathen. It has assumed the work in behalf of women and girls in all our mission fields, and is maintaining schools for girls in India, China and Japan. It has sent a medical missionary to Amoy, and proposes to provide a hospital and dispensary there for the treatment of women. The receipts of this Board reported in 1888, were $17.535. Undoubtedly, the most important movements in Foreign Missions lately made by the Church have been the establishment of a Professorship of Theology in India, for which, through the untiring efforts of the Rev. Dr. Chamberlain, $65.000 were collected through the Church ; and the election of Rev. William W. Scudder, D.D., by the General Synod of 1888. "Professor of Theology in the Theological Seminary in the Arcot Mission." Should not the Church devote herself largely to the work of raising up a native ministry in India, China and Japan, and is not this action an indication that she has begun so to consider it ?

CHAPTER VI.

THE DOCTRINAL STANDARDS.

The great principle of the Reformation is that the Word of God is the only and infallible rule of faith and practice. The Reformers rejected the vain traditions of Rome, and bade all men to come to the living Word, and to search it for themselves. Nevertheless, they composed catechisms and confessions of faith, and attached great importance to them. They never claimed for these, an authority co-ordinate with that of Scripture, but always asserted that everything must be tried by the law and testimony.

It does not follow that, since creeds and confessions have no ultimate authority, they are useless, or even hurtful as snares to truth-loving and conscientious minds. They are useful as bonds of union, as expressions of views in which a number agree, and which therefore furnish a basis for association in visible Church fellowship and work. Even in Churches which discard creeds, there must be an agreement on negations if nothing more, and there can hardly fail to be also an agreement in some positive views, which may not be written or subscribed, but are well understood. In the Bible, Divine truths are introduced in narratives, parables, discussions, precepts, proverbs and prayers, which in a creed, are brought together in an orderly and comprehensive summary, so that we at once see their unity and harmony. Catechisms are of especial value for instruction and edification.

The era of the Reformation was prolific in confessions of faith and catechisms for the instruction of the young. Of these, the oldest is the Augsburg confession, composed by Melancthon, for the Lutheran communion, and this was followed by the numerous confessions and catechisms of the various Protestant Churches.

The agreement of all these confessions on the fundamental articles of Christian doctrine is remarkable, and worthy of the consideration of the Romanist who is accustomed to reproach Protestantism for its variations. A harmony of confessions was early published at Geneva by the Reformed Churches of France and Belgium. Parts of it have been republished in connection with Dr. Thomas Scott's translation of the history of the Synod of Dort.

The doctrinal standards of our Reformed Church are three fold.

I. The Confession of Faith, called the Belgic.

II. The Heidelberg Catechism and the abridgment of it, called the Compendium of the Christian religion.

III. The Canons of the Synod of Dordrecht.

These symbols of doctrine were composed by different persons, under different circumstances and with different ends in view, and so they differ in their characteristics.

The Belgic Confession is a complete, systematic view of the doctrines of the Reformation.

The Heidelberg Catechism is an admirable "Method of instruction in the Christian religion," delineating a true believer's experience and life. The abridgment of it called the "Compendium," was prepared "for the instruction of those who intend to approach the Holy Supper of the Lord."

The Canons of the Synod of Dort are the precise and carefully expressed views of that Synod on the five points of doctrine in controversy between the **Remonstrants** and Contra-Remonstrants.*

I. THE CONFESSION OF FAITH.

This is called the Belgic Confession, from the fact that its author, Guido de Bres, who suffered martyrdom for the truth, was a Belgian. The Reformation very early made great progress in Southern Netherlands or Belgium, and that country furnished its full share of martyrs. The military leaders of Spain, and the inquisitors there had their head-quarters and full sway. The Reformation was arrested in these provinces, and the Protestant inhabitants fled to Northern Netherlands, and strengthened their brethren in the Seven Provinces, and so it happened that Belgium became as thoroughly Papal as any country in Europe.

De Bres, having composed this confession in 1559, submitted it for criticism to Saravia, Calvin, and other eminent divines. Calvin highly approved of it, but suggested that it would be better for the churches of the Netherlands to accept the confession based on a draft by himself, which the French churches had just adopted. But this recommendation was not followed. It was published in 1561 under the title, "Confession de 'foy faicte d'un commun accord, par les eglises, qui sont dispersees en pais-bas." It was at once translated from the French into the Low Dutch; was received with general favor; was adopted by a Synod held at Antwerp in 1566, and by successive Synods of the "churches sitting under the cross," and was finally confirmed by the Synod

*See sermon by the Rev. Dr. A. P. Van Gieson in the "Centennial discourses," p. 243; also paper by the same read before the Conference on Union, at Philadelphia, April 3, 1888.

of Dort in 1619. The Reformed Dutch churches in America have never been without it. Its authority was acknowledged in the Articles of Union in 1772, and subscription to it has been required from every minister to the present day.

This Confession opens with the doctrine of God as One clothed with all perfections; of the means whereby He is made known, viz., Nature and Revelation; of the inspiration of the Bible, its contents, its internal evidence and its sufficiency as a rule of faith, which is declared in article 7, as follows: " We believe that these Holy Scriptures fully contain the will of God, and that whatsoever a man ought to believe unto salvation is sufficiently taught therein. Neither may we compare any writings of men, though ever so holy, with these Divine Scriptures; nor ought we to compare custom, or the great multitude, or antiquity, or succession of times, or persons, or councils, decrees or statutes with the truth of God, for the truth is above all." Thus is the Romish doctrine of the authority of tradition utterly discarded.

We then have statements and proofs of the doctrines of the Trinity; of the Divinity of the Son and of the Holy Spirit; of the creation of all things by God, and of Divine Providence. We are taught that God has left nothing to chance, but that He rules and governs everything " according to His holy will, so that nothing happens in this world without His appointment; nevertheless, God is neither the author of, nor can He be charged with, the sins which are committed."

We are taught that man was created good and holy; that being tempted he fell, and became corrupted through his whole nature; that this corruption has extended to the whole race; that there is no remedy for it but in God's grace; that He displays His mercy and justice, mercy in saving some and justice in inflicting deserved punishment on others; that He has given His own Son to be a Saviour, who became incarnate, was very God and very man, stood as our surety and as a great High Priest brought in an everlasting righteousness. Receiving Him by faith we become justified, and in our justification are included the forgiveness of sins and the setting of Christ's righteousness to our account.

Intimately connected with this justifying faith is the renewal of the man, leading to a new life, and to the production of good works. These are exhibited as unfailing fruits of faith, and results of the work of the Spirit, and so giving proof of that work; but never as the ground of our acceptance with God. This is followed by the statement of the abolition of the ceremonial law, and the full and beautiful and touching article on the intercession of Christ.

Concerning the Church, it is declared that it is "one catholic or universal Church, which is an holy congregation of true Christian believers." It has been from the beginning and will be to the end of the world; all are bound to join themselves to this true Church, which is known by the maintenance of pure Gospel doctrine, pure administration of the sacraments and the exercise of discipline. Hypocrites belong not to the Church, though externally connected with it. The true and false Church and the true and false members are admirably distinguished. In short, the view of the Church given in this article is entirely opposed to the popish and high-church view of the necessity of a certain external organization to the being of the Church. And yet, the necessity of officers and government is admitted, and it is claimed that government by ministers, elders and deacons is in accordance with Holy

Scripture. But these officers are to remember that they are to administer the affairs of Christ's Church in accordance with His will, and that "all human inventions, and all laws which man would introduce into the worship of God, thereby to bind and compel the conscience in any way whatever" are to be rejected.

In regard to the sacraments, it is taught that they have no efficacy of themselves, but that they are visible signs and seals of invisible grace, instituted by Christ and made efficacious by the power of the Holy Spirit. Baptism represents the washing of regeneration and is to be applied to infants of believers by virtue of the Abrahamic covenant. In the Holy Supper, Christ is signified by the bread and wine; and as these elements are received by the mouth, so is Christ received by faith for the nourishment of the soul, and thus the believer is certified of God's love and faithfulness. No air of mystery is thrown over this ordinance, but it is represented as a holy feast in remembrance of Christ, and intended to bind us by faith more closely to Him.

Parts of the article on magistrates are to be interpreted in the light of the sentiments and practice of the age when Church and State were united. All references "to the immediate authority and interposition of the magistrate in the government of the Church" are omitted from our present Church constitution.*

The concluding article declares the facts of the final general judgment; the eternal glory of the righteous and everlasting misery of the wicked.

---

* "Whatever relates to the immediate authority and interposition of the magistrate in the government of the Church, and which is introduced more or less into all the national establishments in Europe, is entirely omitted in the constitution now published." Preface to the Constitution of 1792.

THE HEIDELBERG CATECHISM.

This catechism was received by the churches in the Netherlands about the same time as the confession of faith. Of all the catechisms prepared by Lutheran or Reformed divines, none obtained a greater or more

durable reputation than the Heidelberg. It was composed in the part of Germany known as the Palatinate and by order of its pious and excellent sovereign, the Elector Frederick III. The contention between the Lutherans and the Reformed was, at the time, carried on in his dominions with disgraceful bitterness. The Elector himself adopted the views of the Reformed, and he deemed it to be his duty to introduce a new catechism for the instruction of his people, to be adopted and used by all ministers and in all the churches and schools. This was fully in accordance with the undisputed idea of the age that the State must have a religion to be protected and supported against all others, and that it was an important duty of a sovereign to provide such religion. He hoped by this means, not only to put an end to open dissensions, but also to secure the unity of the churches, and in due time unanimity of views among his people. He engaged two theologians, Caspar Olevianus, Court preacher, and Zacharias Ursinus, Professor in the University of Heidelberg, to prepare a suitable catechism. Having been prepared by them and approved by the Convention of Superintendents, it was published with an introduction by the Elector early in 1563. It met at once with violent opposition from High Lutherans and Romanists, but by the Reformed Churches of all countries it was received with extraordinary favor. Switzerland at once received it, and France, Scotland, England, Poland and Hungary made translations of it into their own languages, and numerous commentaries on it have been written.

Bullinger wrote to a friend: "I have read the catechism of the Elector Palatine Frederick, with the greatest interest, and have blessed God while doing so, who thus perfects His own work. The arrangement of the book is clear; the matter is true and beautiful and good. All is full of light, and faithful and pious. With the greatest brevity, its contents are manifold and large. In my judgment, no better catechism has heretofore been published." *

But from no source has the Heidelberg Catechism received such honor as from the Reformed Church of the Netherlands. It was approved by the Synod of Wesel, in 1568, only five years after its first publication in the Palatinate. Its use was enjoined by the Provincial Synod of Dort, in 1574, and by the National Synod of Dort, 1619. The division into fifty-two Lord's days, which had been made in the Palatinate, was adopted by the Church of the Netherlands, so that the public exposition of it might be completed in the course of every year.

"Her temples," says another, "have resounded with its exposition, and her children have been imbued with its truths for nearly three centuries. The solid bulwarks which the learning of her Altings, and Hornbeeks, and Hommiuses, and Van Tyls, and a host of other eminent divines, have thrown up around the Protestant faith were erected even to the uttermost buttress and escarpment on the outline of the catechism. The heartiness with which she adopted it, and the predominance which her free institutions and her vast opulence and power, as well as the learning of her divines and

---

*Nevin's History of the Heidelberg Catechism, page 86.

schools gave her in the seventeenth century, contributed largely to the unparalleled prominence and diffusion
of this, her favorite symbol. Holland was indebted
to a pure and living faith for strength to stand up
against the most fearful odds ever, perhaps, successfully encountered by a nation, and ultimately to wrest
her liberties from the iron grasp of Philip II., and she
sought with grateful ardor to repay the debt. She
poured it into the minds of the youth who resorted
from far to her universities and schools of theology.
She taught it to the exiles from England, Scotland,
France, and Germany, whom her heroic arm sheltered
from persecution. She sent it to her colonies in the
East and West Indies, and in fine, she, too, transmitted
it with her emigrant children to America, to experience
a freer and wider diffusion after the decay of her own
liberties, and, it must be added, the decline of her own
piety in the Old World." *

The Heidelberg differs from most other catechisms
in this, that it is an account of the comforting experience
of a true believer, and not an abstract system of Christian doctrine. The excellent catechisms of the Westminster Assembly are admirable compends of dogmatic
Theology, while the Heidelberg excels as a delineation
of personal, experimental and practical religion. "The
one is a man's catechism, the other a believer's catechism." The key-note of the one is in its first question,
"What is the chief end of man?" That of the other
is also in its first question, "What is thy only comfort
in life and death?"

The plan of the Catechism is substantially the same
as that of the Epistle to the Romans. After an introduc-
tory question and answer, it treats of the three following subjects:

*Princeton Review, January, 1852.

I.   Of the Misery of Man: Lord's days 2—4.
II. Of Man's Deliverance: Lord's days 5—31.
III. Of Thankfulness: Lord's days 32—52.

Under the first head are treated the following subjects: The law of God as the revealer of sin; the state of integrity; the origin and extent of human depravity, and God's justice in the punishment of the sinner.

Under the second head, it is maintained that Divine justice must be satisfied; that no man can make satisfaction for himself, nor can any creature do it for him; that only, one who is both God and man can make this satisfaction; and that hence the Lord Jesus Christ is the only mediator, as the Scriptures teach us. The provision made by him is sufficient for all sinners, and yet all will not be actually saved, but only those who are ingrafted into Christ and receive him by true faith.

After a beautiful description of faith, the chief doctrines which faith receives are expounded, and they are those which are found in the twelve Articles of the Apostolic Creed. This exposition is followed by a view of the doctrine of justification by faith alone, and a vindication of it from the charge that it makes men careless and profane. Then follow several Lord's days on the Sacraments in which the same views are given as in the Belgic Confession. This part of the Catechism is appropriately concluded with an explanation of the authority in the visible Church to exercise Christian discipline on members who err from the faith or lead wicked lives, so that they may be brought to repentance and be saved.

In the third part of the Catechism it is shown how the believer expresses his gratitude to God for his deliverance. Acknowledging that his good works are not meritorious, he yet confesses his obligation to perform them, and declares that men who lead wicked and ungrateful lives cannot be saved. Thus is conversion insisted on, in which are embraced the mortification of the old man and the quickening of the new, resulting in the performance of good works from a principle of faith and in accordance with the law of God, since only such are entitled to be called good works. The remainder of the Catechism is given to an exposition of the ten Commandments as a rule of life, and of the Lord's Prayer as a comprehensive model to assist us in our daily devotions. The obedience that is required of every Christian leading the Christian life, is not presented on the ground of his natural relation to God as a creature and subject, but, on that of heart-felt gratitude as a chosen child of grace. He is represented as in harmony with the law, which is written by the Spirit of God on his heart.

The requirement to make a complete, annual exposition of this Catechism from the pulpit, was observed in this country until the adoption of the revised constitution in 1833, by which a longer time was allowed to complete the exposition, but not to exceed four years.

The Compendium of the Christian religion is an abridgment of the Heidelberg Catechism, made by the Rev. Herman Faukelius for the use of his church at Middleburg, in Zeeland, which was adopted by the Synod of Dort, and directed by it to be used by the ministers for the instruction of "those who intend to approach the Holy Supper of the Lord."

The Belgic Confession and Heidelberg Catechism were, for fifty years, the only doctrinal standards possessed by the Reformed Church of the Netherlands. Then were added the Canons of the Synod of Dort.

THE CANONS OF THE SYNOD OF DORDRECHT
OR DORT.

These were formulated and adopted by the Synod as expressive of the views of the members on the opinions of the Remonstrants, touching the five points in controversy. It is hoped that our readers will carefully examine them. Perhaps they will find some ground for the remark of the commentator, Rev. Thomas Scott, when he speaks of "the holy, guarded and reverential manner in which the divines of this reprobated Synod stated and explained these doctrines, compared with the superficial and incautious, and often unholy and presumptuous manner of too many in the present day." It must be remembered that there is a distinction between what is called high Calvinism and moderate Calvinism, or in theological phrase, supra-lapsarianism and infra-lapsarianism, the former regarding God as decreeing to make man, and to cause him to fall, etc; the latter, viewing man as fallen, and God as decreeing out of His sovereign pleasure to save some from ruin, and to leave others to the just punishment of their sins. The latter is the view of the Canons, which were so constructed that the members of the Synod, coming from various countries and holding various types of the doctrine, might all be able to subscribe them in good faith and without compromise, and they did unanimously subscribe them.*

I. The first Head of Doctrine treats of Predestination which, according to the Articles, is not, as is often

* "The Reformed Churches in the Netherlands, France. the Palatinate, the greater part of Switzerland, and the Puritans in Great Britain, received these Canons as the scientific and precise statement of Christianty." Shedd's History of Christian Doctrine, Vol. II., p. 477.

represented, God's determination to create some men to be damned, whether they repent or not, for it is very plainly taught that only they perish who deserve it on account of their sin and impenitence. Men are contemplated as in a state of condemnation, and entirely dependent on God's interposition for deliverance from the impending doom. Out of the world of condemned sinners, God, of His sovereign pleasure and mercy chooses to save some, while the others are left in the "common misery into which they have wilfully plunged themselves." The saved are debtors to electing grace, while those who perish receive the deserved punishment of their sins.

The Arminian also holds to divine election, but he denies that it springs from God's sovereign pleasure irrespective of any good in the persons elected, and he maintains on the contrary, that it is based on foreseen faith, repentance and good works. But the Scripture represents men to be elected to faith, sanctification and life.

The common objection that the doctrine of predestination interferes with man's liberty and responsibility cannot be maintained, because no man can prove that these are irreconcilable. He can do no more than assert his own inability to harmonize them, and he has no right to speak for higher intelligences; and least of all, to dispute with God. As a matter of fact, there are no stronger advocates for the claim that man is free to act according to his will, than the most uncompromising champions of the doctrine of Divine sovereignty. And, in truth, every man feels and knows that he follows his own will in sinning and in obeying, and that he is responsible. No man is sensible of the constraining force of God's decree. Divine sovereignty presides over all our affairs, even the minutest; yet, who is fettered by it in word or act? There are great difficulties connected with this view, but no greater than those that encompass the opposite. We must remember that we are not competent to sit in judgment on the ways of the Almighty, and when disposed to do it, should call to mind the admonition of Paul, "Nay, but O man, who art thou, that thou repliest against God?"

This doctrine is not to be made a constant subject of preaching, nor to be presented in a harsh manner, but it is "to be published in due time and place in the Church of God, for which it was peculiarly designed, provided it be done with reverence, in the spirit of discretion and piety, for the glory of God's most holy name, and for enlivening and comforting His people, without vainly attempting to investigate the secret ways of the Most High." *

II. The second head of doctrine treats of "the death of Christ, and the redemption of men thereby." The Arminians held that Christ died in exactly the same sense for all men, and that God is in a certain sense reconciled to all. But in these Articles we are taught that "the death of the Son of God is the only and most perfect sacrifice and satisfaction for sin; is of infinite worth and value, abundantly sufficient to expiate the sins of the whole world;" that its benefits are freely and sincerely offered to all, with the promise that whosoever believeth shall not perish. Nevertheless, Christ had, in dying, a special reference, as the surety of His people, to their salvation. He did not intend merely to open a door by which all might enter and be saved, but also to secure the entrance and salvation of many.

---

*First head of Doctrine, Art. 14. See also conclusion of the Canons.

So he effectually redeems His chosen out of every "people, tribe, nation and language."

III. and IV. The third and fourth heads of doctrine treat of "the corruption of man, his conversion to God, and the manner thereof." The Calvinist and Arminian both believe in the corruption of man's nature and of the need of God's grace for his renovation. The Calvinist regards man as so thoroughly depraved that without special grace he will never turn to God, but will persevere and perish in his wickedness, while those who are saved are debtors to special and distinguishing mercy. God as a sovereign, acts according to His own good pleasure in selecting the subjects of His grace, and effects their regeneration by the bestowment of special Divine influences. The Spirit, with His effectual call, accompanies the external call of the word, and causes a willing and joyous acceptance of offered grace. Yet the submission is not forced and reluctant, for men are made willing in the day of God's power.

The Arminian says that God has given common grace to all men, which one needs only to improve, and which every man is competent to improve. According to this the converted man is one who has improved the grace given to him in common with all others ; the unconverted man, one who has not. The Spirit, according to this view, does not work with such power as to control the will of man, but in conversion, the will falls in with the suggestion of the Spirit, which, nevertheless, it did not need to do.

V. The fifth head of doctrine is the perseverance or preservation of the saints.

There is no question concerning the inevitable result if a converted man should be left to himself. All admit that he must fall in the moment that the Divine help is withdrawn. Moreover, no one denies that a renewed man is, through the power of temptation, and his own weakness, liable to fall into grievous sins which cannot but be offensive to God, and for which he receives correction. But these Articles affirm that God does not utterly take away His Spirit from His renewed ones so that they perish. He preserves the incorruptible seed, renews the erring to repentance, brings them through every difficulty, blesses His ordinances and dispensations to them, so that they are kept unto the end, when they receive the unfading crown.

The Arminian, on the contrary, holds that there is no guarantee for the final salvation of a believer; that "it is possible for the true believer to fall away from true faith, and to fall into sins of such a description as cannot consist with a true and justifying faith; nor is it only possible for them thus to fall, but such lapses not unfrequently occur. True believers are capable, by their own fault, of falling into flagrant crimes and atrocious wickedness, to persevere and die in them, and therefore, finally, to fall away and perish.*

The Confession of Faith, Catechism and Canons, of the contents of which this meagre synopsis has been given, may be found in our hymn-books, and are thus accessible to all; and they are precisely the same as when they were confirmed by the Synod of Dordrecht in 1619.

In connection with this account of the doctrinal standards we remark:

1. That the Reformed Church is not illiberal or exacting in the terms of communion. In the Compendium which was prepared "for those who intend to approach the Holy Supper of the Lord," the fundamental truths of the Gospel are presented in a very simple

---

*Articles of the Remonstrants.

manner and without perplexing metaphysical distinctions. According to the good custom of the times, the
children having been baptized, were, at the proper age,
placed under catechetical instruction, and they were
required to " know and confess the fundamental truths "
contained in this compendium before they could be
admitted to the Lord's Supper. Now, it does not seem
reasonable that a knowledge of, and assent to a larger
body of formulated doctrine should have been required
of an unbaptized adult as a pre-requisite to full communion than was required of one who had been baptized
in infancy, and had received catechetical instruction,
and desired to become a communicant. Why should
there be two different standards of qualification for
these two classes of applicants? Besides, the question
which is in the Form proposed to the adult candidate is
not : Dost thou assent to all the Articles of the Christian
religion as they are contained in the doctrinal standards,
but "as they are taught here in this Christian church,
according to the Word of God?" The question is to be
interpreted by the light of the teaching system of the
Church, and of the immediate object of the teaching.
The object is full communion, and with it this preparatory teaching terminated. It is all comprised in this
compendium of "necessary and fundamental truths."
But Christian instruction could and must, after that, go
on indefinitely for edification. Therefore the Heidelberg catechism was added, to be taught in advanced
catechetical classes, and also to be expounded to the
whole congregation from the pulpit on the Lord's day ;
the teaching element, moreover, is an important one
in all the preaching, and the most advanced Christians
continue to be learners. And besides, it is creditable
to any minister to give much of his time and strength
to the systematic education of his people in matters,
religious, Biblical and ecclesiastical.

The minister, in reading the Form for Adult Baptism, reminds the candidate that he has been privately, that is, personally instructed by him in the Christian religion; but surely he does not mean to say by this, that he has taken him through a system of theology or even that he has gone over all the standards of doctrine held by the Church of which he is a minister. An understanding of and subscription to those standards are very properly required of ministers, for they are teachers of the flock, and they have been set for the defense of the Gospel. But private members are regarded as learners, and a willingness to learn is of more value than an extensive knowledge of formulated doctrine, especially if a docile spirit be lacking.

If it should be claimed, as it sometimes is, that no doctrinal test whatever should be applied in the cases referred to, but that every one should be received to the sacraments whom it is believed Christ would receive, we reply that this statement is misleading. How is it possible to avoid doctrinal tests to some extent? How can a man give evidence of his being a Christian without showing some knowledge of Christianity, or in other words, of the distinctive truths of the Christian religion? No true pastor can converse with an anxious enquirer without at once unfolding the great fundamental truths of the Gospel, and he cannot decide on the credibility of one's Christian profession without a knowledge of his views about essential truths. Every faithful and prudent Christian minister, no matter to what branch of the Church he belongs, does, in his conversations with applicants for admission to the sacraments, continually pass in review the fundamental truths which are found in the Compendium, for this little catechism contains no denominational peculiarities, but only essential truths held in common by believers in the Lord Jesus Christ as a Divine Saviour. Therefore, we claim that when a minister of the Reformed Church requires the candidate for adult baptism to give his "assent to all the articles of the Christian religion, as they are taught in this Christian Church," and to "reject all heresies and schisms repugnant to this doctrine," he asks no more than faithful ministers of other Christian Churches require from those who seek admission at their hands to the holy sacraments; and that he can also rest in the assurance that he is in accord with the historical sense of the question and with the uniform practice which the ministers of the Reformed Church have followed for centuries.*

2. Our system of doctrine is in accord with those of other evangelical, orthodox Churches, as the Episcopal, Presbyterian, parts of the Congregational and Baptist and other Churches.

3. It is reasonable. It is not free from mysteries for no system is. But this seems to be as philosophical and as free from objections as any. Its whole tendency is to exalt God and abase sinful man, which is no mean proof of its truth.

4. It is scriptural. This, if true, should settle the question. The appeal is made to the law and testimony, and to the teaching of prophets, apostles, and the Son of God Himself. This system contains no stronger lan-

---

*"The prerequisites for such communion as stated in the "Directory for worship" of the Presbyterian Church are "knowledge and piety," the how much and the what, men of various graces do, and must determine. And as various as the sessions, are the measures and qualities of the different churches. Liturgical Churches have measures and models to determine these questions. Ours is the Evangelical, Presbyterian, Liturgical Church." Report to the Classis of Paramus, April, 1885.

guage than they used in setting forth the sovereignty, of God in grace as well as in nature.

5. It accords with Christian experience. The believer, of every country and church and creed gives thanks to God for having done in him and for him what he could not do in and for himself. Men contend for opinions and dispute about creeds, and then join in the same expressions of dependence on Divine grace and of thanksgiving for electing love.

6. It promotes holiness of life. In Paul's day it was objected to the doctrine of salvation by grace alone, that it led to licentiousness; but how ably did he vindicate it from the charge, and show that so far from nullifying the law it completely established it, and besides, he and his fellow-disciples gave practical proof of this in their own devoted lives. Similar charges have, in every age, been brought against the doctrines of grace but the men who have held these doctrines have been men of whom the world was not worthy. Cherishing the doctrines of grace as the apple of the eye, they have walked close with God, denying themselves all ungodliness and worldly lusts and living soberly, righteously and godly. And so we preach the humbling doctrine of salvation by God's free grace, assured that all desired reforms in individual character or social life will follow in its train.

7. God has honored this truth and put His seal upon it by using it for the revival of His work. Its central doctrine of justification by faith awakened the new life of the Reformation, a doctrine that must always be the effective emancipator of the individual man from all priestly bondage, for it allows nothing to come in between him and the Christ. This system of evangelical truth produced such marvels in Switzerland, Germany, Holland, France, Scotland and England. What

doctrines did Whitefield and Venn, and Hervey and Berridge and Romaine preach in the last century in England with glorious success, and what were the doctrines of our Edwards and Davies and the Frelinghuysens and Tennents when God accompanied their preaching with such marvelous power? They were the doctrines of native depravity, regeneration by the Spirit, and dependence on the sovereign grace of God for salvation.

We venture to say that revivals are of little worth which would find a disturbing element or a hindrance in these doctrines. They are most serviceable in bringing the sinner to a sense of his need of a Saviour, and to entire reliance upon Him. The Reformed Church is no foe to revivals. She has often enjoyed days of glorious refreshing and ingathering, and so has become wary of spurious excitements, which can so easily be produced if men are willing to use questionable arts and measures, but which are so desolating in their effects, seen in the withering of every green thing, and the resemblance of a church to a field over which the fire has passed. How different the work when God's living truth is honored as the sword of the Spirit, and the Spirit uses it, and many retire to weep in secret places, and enter, with earnest purpose, into solemn covenant with God. These are blessed seasons to be longed and prayed for; seasons of God's visits to His heritage owning and blessing His own truth, and honoring His own appointed means of grace.

8. This form of doctrine is and has ever been the foundation of civil liberty. It was the support of the republic at Geneva. Bancroft denominates Calvinism, "gradual republicanism," and calls Geneva, "the fertile seed-plot of democracy."* It is a doctrinal system

---

*Bancroft's Miscellanies.

Geo. W. Bethune

which kingly tyrants have always dreaded, for it claims the right of private judgment in behalf of every man. It led the Huguenot to resist the dragonnades of the French tyrant, and Holland to prolong the contest with Philip, and Scotland to dye her fields with the blood of her own sons. It led the Puritans of England to stand up against kingly and churchly power, and when a place for the practice and nurture of their principles was denied them in the Old World, these stern, unyielding men came to the New, to establish "a Church without a bishop, and a State without a king."

If we desire the perpetuity of our free institutions, let us know that all depends on the maintenance of the truth as found in the inspired word. This, like leaven, must pervade the whole mass. Then will God appoint unto us salvation for bulwarks.

CHAPTER VII.

LITURGY, CUSTOMS AND USAGES.

The Reformed Church in America is distinguished from the Presbyterian Church of this country by the possession and partial use of an authorized Liturgy, the latter Church having simply a Directory of Worship, without prescribed form or model for any service.

The Liturgy as revised, approved by the Classes and adopted in 1878, rearranged and published in 1882 and recommended by the Synod for use in the churches, contains: I. Order of Scripture lessons. II. Order of public worship: 1. Morning; 2. Evening. III. Prayers for special occasions. IV. The Creeds. V. The administration of Baptism: 1. To infants; 2. To adult persons. VI. The public reception into full communion of those who have been baptized in infancy. VII. The administration of the Lord's Supper. VIII. Church discipline: 1. Excommunication; 2. Readmission of excommunicated persons. IX. Ordination: 1. Of ministers of God's word; 2. Of elders and deacons. X. The installation of a minister. XI. The laying of a corner-stone. XII. The dedication of a house of worship. XIII. The confirmation of marriage. XIV. The burial of the dead.

From this Liturgy is omitted the office for the consolation of the sick, which was entitled in Dutch, " Den Ziekentroost," and in English, " The consolation of the sick, which is an instruction in faith, and the way of salvation, to prepare believers to die willingly." This was a simple, scriptural view of the process of man's salvation from its beginning in regeneration to its completion in glory, and was doubtless prepared as a help to the "Kranken-besoeeker," or "Zieken-trooster," in his visitations of the sick. In all editions of the Liturgy that have been published for many years past, this office has consisted entirely of classified references to passages of Scripture. The authority for substituting these for the original, full and very suggestive office, does nowhere appear, nor does the authority for the later omission of this substituted form appear.

The Liturgy as published in 1882, was recommended by the General Synod for use in the churches; but by the Constitution of the Church, the use of the following is made imperative, viz: The forms for the administration of Baptism and the Lord's Supper; the forms for the ordination of ministers, elders and deacons; and the forms for the excommunication of offenders, and for the readmission of penitents. Every minister, when installed as pastor, binds himself to obey the Constitution, and therefore to use these forms on the occasions for which they have been provided.

The forms of prayer contained in the Liturgy are not used by our ministers in ordinary public worship, though they are at liberty to use them if so disposed. The Church believes in the lawfulness of forms of prayer, and that there are occasions when their use is profitable and expedient. She on the one hand rejects the extreme view that prayer cannot be acceptable unless the words are immediately dictated by the Holy Ghost, and on the other, the view that it is presumptuous to pray in public worship, except in the language of a prescribed form. She finds no command of Scripture binding the ministry or Church to the use of such forms, nor does the example of Christ make it imperative, nor does it appear that the apostles or primitive

Christians confined themselves to imposed forms of prayer. It has been said by one that their usual practice was, " First, to begin with the Lord's Prayer, as the ground and foundation of all others, and then, according to their circumstances and conditions, to offer up their own prayers and requests. Now these other prayers, which made up a great part of Divine service, were not stinted and imposed forms, but the words and expressions of them were left to the prudence, choice and judgment of every particular bishop or minister." He further says " I do not here say that a bishop or minister used no arbitrary form of prayer—all that I say is, that there was none imposed. Neither do I say, that having no imposed form, they unpremeditatedly, immethodically or confusedly vented their petitions and requests, for, without doubt, they observed a method in their prayers; but this is what I say—that the words or expressions of their prayers were not imposed or prescribed; but every one that officiated, delivered himself in such terms as best pleased him, and varied his petitions according to the present circumstances and emergencies, or if it be more intelligible, that the primitive Christians had no stinted liturgies or imposed forms of prayer."*

The question with us is, not about the lawfulness of the use of precomposed forms of prayer, but about the expediency of their prescription or imposition for all occasions. The history of our Church is, from its begining throughout, a testimony against the latter. While forms, to some extent, have been required to be used, and some have been recommended as models, the officiating minister has always been allowed a large liberty in the composing and offering of prayers. Great impor-

---

*Lord King's Primitive Church, Part II., Chap. 2.

tance has been attached to the education of ministers,
so that they might be able to pray as well as preach
to edification. It is rightly expected of them that they
shall not pray extemporaneously, in the popular sense
of the word, that is, without preparation, but that they
shall make very careful preparation for this part of
public service, as well as for preaching.* This should
be made by every minister in the way that seems best
to him, by a careful review of circumstances, arrangement of topics and thoughts, formation of sentences,
or even the writing out of the whole prayer, to be read,
or not, in the pulpit. It would be well for young ministers for a long time to practice themselves in devotional composition, especially of their public prayers.
Dr. Witherspoon recommended devotional composition to his theological students, and President Ashbel
Green, of Princeton College, who had been one of these
students, says of himself, that in the early part of his
ministry, he wrote his prayers as regularly as he did
his sermons, and he expressed his regret that ministers generally made so little preparation for conduct-
ing the devotional exercises of the congregation.   Dr.
Gillies, of Glasgow, for the first ten years of his pastoral life, never composed a sermon without writing a
prayer in connection with it. Careful preparation of
some sort for public prayer may not, without guilt, be
neglected by him who is the mouth of the congregation.

This liberty is contended for, because a prescribed
Liturgy without any liberty at all, can never fully meet
the wants of the Church, for it must often lack adapt-
ation to changing circumstances. The prayer composed
by a minister for an occasion, may not be as good a

*This is also insisted on in the Westminster Directory of
Worship.
†Jones' Life of Green, p. 545.

piece of devotional composition, as one that has come down to us from past ages, but it may be better adapted to the occasion, just as his sermons may be inferior as compositions to many contained in the works of distinguished divines, yet may be better suited to the times and circumstances. Why should it not be required of him to preach prescribed sermons as well as to pray prescribed prayers?

It may well be asked whether the advantages of both form and freedom might not be enjoyed in public worship. There are confessions, thanksgivings, and petitions that are always appropriate when the people are assembled for worship and which should never be omitted, such as confession of sin, thanks for blessings of Providence and grace, prayers for all classes and conditions of men, the sick, the bereaved, those in authority, etc. These might be embodied in forms to be used by the minister, and so the offering of them would be secured. In connection with this might be prayers in which due notice should be taken of special needs and circumstances, in the offering of which the minister should have unrestricted freedom. The early histories of all the Reformed Churches, including the Church of the Netherlands, prove the practicability of this combination. They did neither dispense with forms, nor confine their ministers to them.

Liturgies were early adopted by the Reformed Churches in Geneva, France, the Palatinate, England, Scotland, and the Netherlands. When the Puritans arose in England, claiming that the Church of England was only half-reformed, and demanding further reforms they were met with persecution. Naturally, they went to the extreme of simplicity in worship, and set their faces against all liturgies, forms, sacred vestments, holy days, kneeling in prayer, etc. The Presbyterians

of Scotland, after having received from the hands of
John Knox a liturgy which was used for some time,
were so outraged by the attempts of England to force
Episcopacy upon them, that they indignantly trampled
all forms and liturgies under foot.* But the Reformed
Churches on the Continent were subjected to no such
influences, and they grew in attachment to their forms
of service.

Calvin's liturgy was the foundation of the liturgy
of the Reformed Church of the Netherlands, which
was not completed at once, but was the result of a gradual growth.† The authorship of its various parts cannot be easily traced. London may, however, be truly
called its cradle. The oppressive measures of Charles
V. and Philip II. against their Protestant subjects in
the Netherlands drove thousands of them into other
countries. Very many of them went to Rhenish Prus-
sia, and many also to Embden, in East Friesland, where
the Reformed Church was planted under the auspices
of John á Lasco, a converted Polish nobleman, Albert
Hardenberg and others. On the accession of Edward
VI. to the throne of England, the eyes of the Reformed
of Continental Europe were turned to that country,
and many went thither from the Netherlands, and many
from the Church of Embden. A church composed of
these emigrants was formed in London, and by royal
authority the Abbey of Austin Friars was given them
for a house of worship, which church is in existence,
and the property in its possession, and worship statedly
held in the Holland tongue, at the present day. These
refugees of the Reformed faith were placed by the

*McCrie's Life of John Knox, p. 430: Baird's Eutaxia, p.
127.

†Henry's Life of Calvin, Vol. I., p. 412, Calvin's Liturgy
was used in preparing the Book of Common Prayer; Eutaxia,
p. 190.

King under the care of á Lasco as superintendent, with whom were associated four other ministers.* The British Reformers took great interest in these refugees, and secured for them many privileges. Á Lasco had come over by express invitation of Cranmer, who gave him a home for six months in the archiepiscopal palace, and who consulted him on the reforms desirable in the Church of England. He was also appointed in 1552, one of the eight divines on the commission to revise the laws of the Church of England.†

When Mary ascended the throne, this congregation was dispersed for a season, but on the accession of Elizabeth, the aspect of affairs changed again, and the church in London was revived and soon numbered more than three thousand members. Churches were also formed in Norwich, Colchester and other places. The Dutch and French refugees introduced many useful manufactures into England, and they became a very important element in the population.‡

The French Protestants in England had somewhat the advantage over the Dutch, for they brought with them the liturgy of Strasburg which had been prepared by Calvin, and which differed very slightly from the Genevan liturgy. This was translated by their pastor, Valerandus Polanus, into Latin for the use of the ministers in London. It was made by á Lasco, the basis for a more extended work, embracing the principles and rules of Church Order as well as forms of worship, but which was not published during his connection

---

*See the charter of this church in the appendix to Burnet's History of the English Reformation.

† Dalton's Johannes á Lasco; Presbyterian Review, January, 1881, Article John á Lasco; Bartel's John á Lasco; á Lasco Opera, edited by Kuypers.

‡Weiss' Hist. of French Prot. Refugees, New York, 1854.

with the church of London. A brief manual was prepared in 1551, by Martin Micron, one of the ministers. This, like the liturgy, was written in Latin, for these works were intended for the use of the ministers rather than the people, and also for the information of the authorities in England, and they remained in manuscript until after the dispersion of the congregation on Queen Mary's accession, when they were printed on the Continent. Meanwhile, a translation of Micron's manual was made into the Dutch language, by Jan Uytenhove, one of the elders, a nobleman of Ghent, who had cast in his lot with these afflicted people of God.* This little book was afterwards published at Embden, and was, for a number of years, used there and in various parts of the Netherlands.

Next came the liturgy of Petrus Dathenus. He was pastor of the refugees from the Netherlands who had gathered by thousands at Frankenthal in the Palatinate, and to whom the Elector granted great privileges. He was a man of rare gifts, of fiery zeal, indomitable perseverance, and a preacher of immense popularity. He prepared forms of worship for his church at Frankenthal, and published in connection with them, a translation of the Heidelberg Catechism in Low Dutch, and a metrical version of the Psalms. These forms were very soon accepted as the authorized liturgy of the churches of the Netherlands, and their use was enjoined on the "Churches under the Cross," by the early Synods. In preparing this liturgy, Dathenus made use of that of the Palatinate, the basis of which was the "Forma ac Ratio" of á Lasco; also, of Calvin's Liturgy and of that of Zurich.

Other forms were subsequently added as occasion

*Pijper's Jan Uytenhove, Leiden, 1883.

required, one of which was the article for the "Consolation of the Sick and Dying." Connected with this liturgy was a short catechism for the examination of those who intended to unite with the church, for which the Compendium was afterwards substituted by the Synod of Dort. This Synod also added the form for the administration of Baptism to adults, which had been provisionally adopted by the Synod of South Holland in 1604.

The Provincial Synod of Dordrecht, 1574, directed all ministers to use the same form of public prayer, and also authorized them at the same time to introduce petitions for special cases relating to the magistracy or to sick persons. The forms of prayer for ordinary worship were never used exclusively, and they gradually went into disuse, while those for the administration of Baptism and the Lord's Supper, and those for the ordination of ministers, elders, and deacons have continued to be used to the present time. The Remonstrants objected, not only to the confession of faith and the catechism, but also to parts of the liturgy, which was revised by a commission of the Synod and was, by the direction of the Synod, published in connection with the standards of doctrine.

The Liturgy was, soon after this, translated into the English language for the use of churches in Holland composed of Scotch and English refugees.* These came into ecclesiastical relationship with the Reformed Church of the Netherlands and therefore needed the liturgy. In 1767, three years after Rev. Dr. Laidlie had begun to officiate in English in the church of New York, an amended edition of this translation was published by the Consistory of that church, which,

* Steven's History of the Scottish Church of Rotterdam, Edinburgh, 1832.

so far as the forms made imperative by the constitution are concerned, has remained unchanged.

These forms begin with a statement of the scriptural authority for the act to be performed and an exposition of its nature, which are followed by such questions or exhortations and prayers as are appropriate. The baptismal form contains an exposition of the doctrine of baptism, with questions to the parents of the infant, or to the adult candidate, and suitable admonitions and prayers. The forms of ordination are constructed on the same principle. In the concluding prayer in all these forms the element of thankfulness predominates.

The form for the administration of the Lord's Supper is worthy of special notice. It opens with the words of institution 1 Cor. 11:23-29 which are followed by the statements that two things are necessary to a profitable use of the Supper, self examination, and a directing of the Supper to the remembrance of Christ; and that in self examination there are three inquiries: 1, Whether we have an humbling sense of personal guilt. 2, Whether we trust that our sins are forgiven for Christ's sake. 3, Whether we propose henceforth to live rightly before God and man. All who can affirmatively answer these questions are accounted worthy partakers.

Then follows the admonition to those who are living scandalous lives to abstain from the Supper, followed by the encouraging assurance to the penitent that though his sins may be numerous and aggravated, he will be received of God and counted worthy, if he is sorry for them and fights against them.

The second part contains an affecting view of Christ's atoning work, and an exhibition of the relation of the Supper to our faith in Him; also a careful directing of the attention away from the elements used to the sacrifice represented by them; and finally, to an exhibition of

the union of believers with one another by virture of
their union with Christ, and of the consequent duty of
brotherly love.

To this succeeds an appropriate prayer which is followed by the Apostolic Creed, which is in many
churches appropriately repeated audibly by the communicants, thus making confession with their "mouths
and hearts." During the communion an appropriate
hymn may be sung or chapter read. After it, thanksgiving is offered chiefly in the language of Psalm 103,
and this is followed with a prayer ending with the
Lord's prayer.

Those who have been accustomed to hear this form
from childhood have become exceedingly attached to it,
and the commendation of it by others is frequent and
hearty. It has sometimes been used by our ministers
in churches of other denominations, greatly to the satisfaction of the communicants. That its excellence may
be fully seen and felt, it must be read in its integrity
by one who appreciates it, and not be abridged and
mutilated according to the caprice of an officiating
minister.

Considerable changes have been made in the order of
worship since the day that the Dutch refugees worshiped in the Church of Austin Friars in the time of
Edward. The following is a description of the order
of worship as then conducted in the church of London:

"The congregation being assembled in their house
of worship, the minister ascended the pulpit and commenced with a brief exhortation to the solemn and
devout observance of worship. Prayer was then offered
according to a prescribed form, the same which is
still found in our liturgy, with the title, 'A prayer
before the explanation of the catechism.' After this
a psalm was sung and the minister preached on a por-

tion of Scripture commonly consisting, not of one, two or three verses, but of a continuous paragraph, or a history standing by itself. Thus the minister illustrated, explained and enforced in several sermons, a whole book of Scripture, as for instance, the Epistle to the Romans in continuance, each sermon or homily occupying about an hour. After this the minister announced what was proper to be announced to the congregation, but only that which respected public worship. Then a prayer was again offered according to a prescribed form which was short and appropriate, and this was followed by the distinct and emphatic reading of the ten commandments, after which the minister exhorted the congregation to confession of sin, and then he offered prayer in penitent confession of sin, and supplication for Divine forgiveness, according to a prescribed form, brief and impressive. After this he read the following declaration : 'Seeing it pleases God to receive in His grace those who are truly penitent and sincerely confess their sins, and on the contrary to leave obstinate sinners who cover and palliate their sins to themselves, I therefore declare from the word of God to the penitent who believe in Christ alone for salvation, that through His merits alone, their sins are forgiven of God, Amen. And to as many as do not confess and forsake their sins, or who, if they confess their sins, seek salvation from any other source than the merits and grace of Christ, and thus love darkness rather than light, I declare from the word of God, that their sins are bound in heaven, until they repent and turn to Christ.' Immediately after this the Apostles' Creed was read as bearing the common confession of their faith, and this was followed by the long or general prayer, either in the prescribed form of the liturgy or else at the discretion of the minister, accommodated to

the wants and circumstances of the church, and concluding with the Lord's prayer. A psalm was then
sung by the whole congregation led by a chorister in
front, near the pulpit. The minister then commended
the wants of the poor to their brethren for alms which
were collected by the deacons at the door of the church
after the benediction had been pronounced according
to the form. 'The Lord bless thee etc.'*

Some changes from this order were made in the
Netherlands when freedom to worship had been
obtained. The clerk or voorleser standing in the bap-
tistery (doophuisje) under the pulpit opened the services
by reading a few texts of Scripture, the ten commandments, and a chapter; after which he read a psalm
and led in the singing of it; tablets also were hung on
the walls indicating the psalms to be sung during the
service. The minister then appeared, and having stood
a few moments at the foot of the pulpit stairs in silent
prayer, entered the pulpit, and made a few remarks
bearing on the subject of the sermon to be delivered, and
this was called the 'Exordium remotum.' This was
followed by prayer, and singing and then the sermon,
which frequently, was an expository lecture in course.
At first the Apostles' Creed was read after the sermon,
but it was soon transferred to the afternoon service.
The sermon in the afternoon was an exposition of one
of the Lord's days of the Heidelberg catechism.

The same order, essentially, was for many years
followed by the Dutch churches in this country. Worship in the church of New York more than a hundred
years ago, is thus described. After the preliminary
services conducted by the voorleser, the domine arose
and made a short prayer in nearly the following words:
'Our only help and powerful support we expect alone

*Ypey en Dermout, Geschiedenis, Vol. I., p. 481.

from Thee, the only and triune God, the Father, the
Son and the Holy Ghost, Creator of the heavens, the
earth, and the seas, and who keepest faith and truth
forever, Amen.' He then commenced his exordium
remotum with the Apostolic salutation, 'Grace, Mercy
and Peace etc.,' and towards the close of it, he often
added, 'But that I may speak, and you may hear, so
that God may be glorified, and our souls edified, it is
above all things necessary at the commencement of our
meeting to bow the knees of our souls, and to call upon
Him who is Spirit, in spirit and in truth, in the following manner." The announcement of the text followed
the prayer, and after a suitable introduction and
explanation of the context, the preacher proceeded to
divide his subject into general heads, and to supplicate
the Divine blessing in a short ejaculation, and then
added 'But before we proceed, we would recommend
unto you the poor and necessitous, whom Christ hath
left in the midst of us, accompanied with a command to
do good unto them; each of you, my friends, give liber-
ally and bountifully, according as God hath blessed you.
Truly think, if it is done from a principle of faith,
that God, who seeth in secret, will reward you openly,
if not in this life in that which is to come, eternally.
The God and Father of all grace and mercy incline
your hands and hearts to a liberal contribution towards
supplying the wants of the necessitous, and may he
awaken your attention to what shall be further spoken.*
During this address, the deacons stood before, and fac-
ing the pulpit, each holding the staff in his hand with
the bag attached for collecting the alms. When the
sermon commenced, the voorzanger turned the hour-

---

*The early Synods of the churches of the Netherlands
repeatedly decreed that sermons should be short, not exceeding
an hour.

glass which stood near him in a brass frame, and if the sermon continued more than an hour, he turned the hour-glass again, and set it in another place that it might be seen that an hour had elapsed.* Immediately after the sermon was ended, the voorzanger arose, and by means of a white rod with a cleft in the end into which the papers were put, handed to the domine the requests of those persons who desire the prayers and thanksgivings of the church; of prayers in cases of sickness or other afflictions, in cases of dangerous sea-voyages etc., of thanksgivings in cases of recovery from dangerous sickness, and in cases of a safe return from sea, etc. At the receipt of these papers, and after examining them, the domine, addressing the congregation, said, 'As we commence with prayer, it is our bounden duty to close with thanksgiving, remembering in our prayers those who have requested the prayers and thanksgivings of the church,' naming the cases in which they had been desired. After the prayer a psalm was sung, and the services were closed with the benediction.†

The order of worship which was authoritatively published in 1882, provides for a restoration of some things that had fallen into disuse, as the repetition of the Apostles' Creed, and for the addition of responsive readings from the Psalter, of responses to the Decalogue, and of reading lessons from both the Old and New Testaments; much of it is not imperative, but optional with any church to adopt or not.

The salutation and benediction which have always maintained their places in the order, are similar to and yet differ from the ordinary prayers in public

*It is the custom in Holland at the present time to collect the alms after the beginning of the sermons.

†Reformed Dutch Church Magazine, Vol. II., p. 275.

worship. In the latter the minister stands as the representative of the people; in the former, as the representative of Christ. As the ambassador of God, he authoritatively blesses the people, or invokes upon them the richest blessings of God's grace. His greeting of them with the salutation is of this character, as is also the dismissal with the benediction. Therefore, the pronoun is to be used in the second person, 'the grace etc., be with you,' not with us. These, though not priestly, are yet official acts, and must not be regarded as empty forms, but significant and solemn parts of Divine service.

Some customs connected with the administration of the sacraments have been changed in the course of time. At first, infant baptism was confined to the children of those who had made an open profession of faith; it was afterward allowed to children of those who had themselves been baptized, and were sound in the faith, and of good moral character. The place of baptism for both infants and adults was the church, unless sickness or some other cause made this impossible or very inconvenient; for baptism was regarded as the sacrament of initiation into the visible Church, and therefore to be administered in the presence of the assembled congregation, and with their united prayer. Our present constitution says, that 'the sacrament of baptism shall, if possible, be administered in the church or some other place of public worship, at the time of public worship.'

Baptism was formerly administered on any Lord's day; now stated times at longer intervals are appointed. But the intervals should not be too long, for successive postponements of the baptism, even for good reasons, sometimes result in the entire neglect of it. Infants were formerly baptized after the sermon, now usually

before it. Sponsors were associated with the parents,
which custom the Synod of Dort declared to be a matter
of indifference, and yet on that very account not to be
causelessly changed. It was directed that in congregations which were accustomed to have sponsors, only
such should be admitted who were sound in the faith
and of exemplary lives. The names of sponsors appear
very regularly on the baptismal records of the old
Dutch churches of this country. Our present constitution has no reference to the subject of sponsors and
in practice they are universally dispensed with; but we
have in one of the questions in our old unchanged form
the words ' parent or witness.' It is universally admitted that an infant may, under certain circumstances, be
presented for baptism by those who are not its parents.
Whether there should be one or three sprinklings has
been declared a matter of indifference. Great care has
been and always should be taken to keep the records of
baptisms accurately, for baptized children are under
the care of the church which engages to assist in their
religious training.

The Lord's Supper was at first observed once in every
two months, which is not too often. Two weeks notice
was given, and a course of family visitations was made
by the minister and elders for the purpose of preparing the members for the approaching solemnity; similar
visitations before or after the communion are still
required by the constitution. A preparatory service
was, as now, held a few days before the communion, at
which time reports were made on the spiritual condition of the congregation, and such discipline as was
needed was exercised.

At the administration the form was read, and the
minister and as many of the members as could, seated
themselves at the table, or surrounded it standing, for

it had been decided very early by the Synods that communicants might sit or stand at the table, sitting being preferred, while the kneeling posture was forbidden as encouraging a superstitious reverence for the elements. These, having partaken, made way for others until all had communed, and in the intervals portions of Scripture were read by the voorleser or a stanza from a hymn was sung. In the earliest period in the Netherlands the communicants, before approaching the table, knelt in their places and with uplifted eyes offered silent prayer; and in the after part of the day a thanksgiving sermon was preached.

The writer has a distinct remembrance of the manner in which the Lord's Supper was administered by the Rev. James V. C. Romeyn in the churches of Hackensack and Schraalenberg. The communicants stood around the table, the aged male members taking precedence, and who were followed by the younger ones. The females followed in the same order, and last of all, the colored members, who were generally slaves. The minister broke the bread as he passed around the table, giving to each one a portion from his own hand, and accompanying the act with some remark or quotation from Scripture, often beautifully appropriate to the particular case. A portion of Scripture was read, or a stanza was sung between the tables.

A very marked characteristic of the Reformed Dutch Church from the first, has been her care for the instruction of the young. She was not only zealous to provide the university for the education of her ministers, but also the parish school for the instruction of the children. Christian nurture was regarded as the chief means for perpetuating the Church. Christian parents were expected to present their children for baptism; to train them for God, and to expect covenanted grace for them, so that at a suitable age they would be led to make a sincere profession of their faith in Christ. She did not depend on periodical excitements, nor even chiefly on conversions of adults from without for an increase of a godly seed, but to the Divine blessing on the careful indoctrination and training of the young in the bosom of the Church. Infant baptism, in connection with such nurture, has an important meaning which is sadly lost sight of in our day. We have gained nothing, but lost much, by exchanging the strong faith of our fathers that God would renew and, through Christian training, sanctify the child, for the vague hope that He will, perhaps, suddenly convert it in mature years. It is true that methods of instruction and training must be adjusted to times and circumstances; but the plan adopted by the Synod of Dort, which was so admirably suited to the times, and yet so clearly presents the principles of Christian education which can never change, must be quoted in full for the benefit of readers who cannot refer to the Acts of the Synod:

" In order that the Christian youth may be diligently instructed in the principles of religion, and be trained in piety, three modes of catechizing should be employed: 1. In the homes by parents. 2. In the schools by schoolmasters. 3. In the churches, by ministers and elders, and catechists especially appointed for the purpose. That these may diligently employ their trust, the Christian magistrates shall be requested to promote, by their authority, so sacred and necessary a work; and all who have the oversight of churches and schools shall be required to pay special attention to this matter.

1. The office of parents is diligently to instruct their children and their whole household, in the principles of the Christian religion, in a manner adapted to their

respective capacities: earnestly and carefully to admonish them to the cultivation of true piety; to engage their punctual attendance on family worship, and to take them with them to the hearing of the Word of God. They should require their children to give an account of the sermons they hear, especially those on the catechism, assign them some chapters of Scripture to read, and certain passages to commit to memory, and then impress and illustrate the truths contained in them, in a familiar manner adapted to the tenderness of youth. Thus they are to prepare them for being catechized in the schools, and by attendance on these to encourage them, and to promote their edification. Parents are to be exhorted to the faithful discharge of their duty, not only by the public preaching of the Word, but specially at the ordinary period of the family visitations, previous to the administration of the Lord's Supper; and also at other proper times by the minister, elders, etc. Parents who profess religion and are negligent in this work shall be faithfully admonished by the ministers, and, if the case requires it, shall be censured by the Consistory that they may be brought to the discharge of their duty.

2. Schools in which the young shall be properly instructed in the principles of Christian doctrine shall be instituted not only in cities, but also in towns and country places where heretofore none have existed. The Christian magistracy shall be requested that well-qualified persons may be employed and enabled to devote themselves to the service, and especially that the children of the poor may be gratuitously instructed, and not be excluded from the benefit of the schools. In this office none shall be employed but such as are members of the Reformed Church having certificates of an upright faith and pious life, and of being well versed in the truths of the Catechism.

They are to sign a document professing their belief in the confession of faith and the Heidelberg catechism, and promising that they will give catechetical instruction to the young in the principles of Christian truth according to the same. The schoolmasters shall instruct their scholars according to their age and capacity, at least two days in the week, not only by causing them to commit to memory, but also by instilling into their minds an acquaintance with the truths of the catechism.

For this end, three forms of the catechism adapted to the three-fold circumstances and ages of the young shall be used. The first shall be for the young children, comprising the Articles of Faith or Creed, the ten Commandments, the Lord's Prayer, the doctrine of the Sacraments and of Church discipline, with some short prayers and plain questions adapted to the three parts of the catechism.

The second shall be a short compendium of the catechism of the Palatinate, or Heidelberg, used in our churches, in which those who are somewhat more advanced than the former shall be instructed. The third shall be the catechism of the Palatinate, or Heidelberg, adopted by our churches for the youth still more advanced in years and knowledge. The Walloon Churches of the Netherlands, who have long been accustomed to the use of the Genevan catechisms, may still continue them in their schools and churches, but the schoolmasters shall not employ any other formularies than these in their schools. The magistrates shall be requested to exclude from the schools all Popish catechisms, and all other books which contain errors and impurities. The schoolmasters shall take care not only that the scholars commit these catechisms to memory, but that they suitably understand the doctrines contained in them. For this purpose they shall suitably explain the topics to every one in a manner adapted to his capacity, and frequently inquire if they are understood. The schoolmasters shall bring every one of the pupils committed to their charge to the hearing of the preached word, and particularly the preaching on the catechism, and require from them an account of the same.

3. In order that due knowledge may be obtained of the diligence of the schoolmasters and the improvement of the youth, it shall be the duty of the ministers, together with an elder, and if necessary, with a magistrate, to visit all the schools, private as well as public, frequently, in order to excite the teachers to earnest diligence, to encourage and counsel them in the duty of catechising, and to furnish an example by questioning them; addressing them in a friendly and affectionate manner, and exciting them to early piety and diligence. If any of the schoolmasters should be found neglectful or perverse, they shall be earnestly admonished by the ministers, and if necessary, by the Consistory in relation to their office. If these exhortations produce no effect, the magistrates shall be requested to exercise their authority in leading them to the discharge of their duty, or to appoint others more qualified and faithful in their places. The ministers in the discharge of their public duty to the Church, shall preach on the catechism.* These sermons shall be comparatively short, and accommodated as far as practicable to the comprehension of children

---

*It was required of every minister that the sermon on Sunday afternoon should be explanatory of one of the Lord's Days of the Heidelberg Catechism so that the whole catechism might be expounded in the course of the year. Our ministers are still required by the Constitution and by their calls to do this work but are allowed to occupy four years with it.

as well as adults. The labors of those ministers will be praiseworthy who diligently search out the wants of country places, and see that catechetical instruction be supplied and faithfully preserved. Experience teaches that the ordinary instruction in the church, catechetical and other, is not always sufficient to instill that knowledge of the Christian religion, which should, among the people of God be well grounded; and also testifies that the living voice has very great influence, and that familiar and suitable questions and answers adapted to the comprehension of each individual is the best mode of catechising, in order to impress the principles of religion upon the heart. It shall be the duty of the ministers to go with an elder to all capable of instruction, and collect them either in their houses, the consistory chamber, or some other suitable place, particularly, a number of those more advanced in years and explain familiarly to them the Articles of the Christian faith, and catechize them according to the circumstances of their different capacities, progress and knowledge. They shall question them on the matter of the public sermons on the catechism. Those who desire to unite with the church shall, three or four weeks before the administration of the Lord's Supper, be frequently and more carefully instructed, that they may be better qualified, and be more free to give a satisfactory account of their faith. The minister shall employ diligent care to ascertain those who give any hopeful evidence of serious concern for the salvation of their souls, and invite them to them, assembling together those who have like impressions, and encourage them to friendly intercourse and free conversation with each other. These meetings shall commence with appropriate prayer and exhortation. If all this shall be done by the ministers with that cordiality, faithfulness, zeal and discretion that become those who must give an account of the flock committed to their charge, it is not to be doubted that in a short time abundant fruit of their labors shall be found in growth in religious knowledge, and holiness of life to the glory of God, and the prosperity of the Church of Christ.*

This system of Christian education was brought with the Church to this country and the schoolmaster was considered to be almost as important as the minister. In new settlements he usually preceded the minister, taught the parochial school in which the catechisms were not neglected, and in his capacity of voorleser conducted public worship, reading the Scriptures, and a sermon, and leading in the singing of psalms. Here, as in Holland, the church and school-house stood side by side, and both were cared for by the consistory. After a season, when the communities became more heterogeneous, the parochial school was superseded by the district common school, in which catechetical instruction could not be permitted, and it was thenceforth confined to the family and the churches.†

In 1809, an unsuccessful attempt was made by the General Synod to revive the whole system of religious instruction that had been established by the Synod of Dort. In 1854 another attempt was made by the General Synod by adopting a plan for parochial schools and recommending their establishment wherever it was deemed practicable. A few schools of this character were at the time established and were successful for a

---

* Acta Synodi Dordrecht, Session XVII.

†The school established in connection with the collegiate church in New York in 1633 is still in existence. See its interesting history by Henry W. Dunshee, second edition published by authority of the Consistory, 1883.

season, being aided in their early history by the munifi-
cence of Mr. Samuel B. Schieffelin of the Collegiate
Church of New York.* The public school system in our
country practically forbids the maintenance to any considerable extent of parochial schools in connection with
Protestant Churches, especially outside of large cities.
Christian people are therefore called to increased diligence in using the other agencies provided for the
religious education of the young.

But though we may not be able to carry out the second
part of the plan of the Synod of Dort, by teaching the
catechism in the day-schools, yet we are committed
to the religious instruction of the young. There is
nothing to prevent heads of families from doing their
duty if so disposed, and they ought to realize that no
privileges which their children enjoy elsewhere can
compensate for the lack of faithful training in the
home. There is now a loud call for the revival of
regular catechetical instruction in the family. Nor
is there anything to prevent ministers and consistories
from doing their duty. Greatly does the pastor err
who is content to have no hold on the young, and who
deems catechetical instruction well enough in a past
age, or even now if convenient, but not of the utmost
importance. An excellent opportunity is afforded by
the Sunday School for officers and members of the
Church, as well as pastors to exercise their gifts in
feeding the lambs of Christ's flock. Consistories should
not allow this precious work to be done by any hands
into which it may happen to fall, but should be as careful in the selection of teachers for the children in
religious truth, as of pastors to teach the congregation from the pulpit.

*Acts and Proceedings of the General Synod, 1854.

THE POETICAL LITURGY.

The poetical Liturgy or service of song has an interesting history. In the Romish Church this part of service was in mediaeval times performed by the priests chanting Latin hymns. The reformers restored it to the people, and versions of the psalms were made into various, vernacular languages, set to music, and sung by the assembled congregations. To the psalms, Luther added hymns in German, expressive of devotional feeling and Christian experience, so that he has been justly called the "Father of modern Hymnology." Calvin, while not an enthusiast in music, like Luther, yet allowed its importance in Church services, introduced the French translations of Marot and Beza into the Church of Geneva and provided for the instruction and training of the congregation, and especially of the young in sacred music.

The earliest metrical translation of the psalms into Dutch was made from the Latin Vulgate in 1539 by William Nieuwveldt, Lord of Bergambacht, etc. These psalms were set to secular melodies, and were popular, but not well suited for public worship. Many editions were published and it continued to be used till the version of Dathenus was adopted by synodical authority. The secular melodies, it was said, secured the singers against the spies and informers by whom they were watched.

Jan Uytenhove, the renowned elder of the church of the refugees in London, completed in 1566 a translation of all the psalms, which he had begun in 1551, and to it he added the songs of Mary, Zacharias and Simeon, the Ten Commandments, the Lord's Prayer, and the Apostolic Creed.

Translations of thirty seven of the psalms were made

from the French of Marot and Beza in 1565, by Lucas De Heere, a painter and poet of Ghent. Appearing only a year before the complete version of Dathenus, they never came into general use.

Clement Marot published translations in French in 1539, of thirty of the psalms. and secular melodies having been fitted to them, they became very popular in France, and were sung at the French Court, until it was discovered that they were heretical, when they were prohibited. Marot afterwards translated twenty more at Geneva, and the remaining hundred were translated by Beza. These were brought from Geneva into the Netherlands and used in the Walloon Churches, having been set to music by Claude Goudimel, Louis Bourgeois, and Claude Le Jeune.

Of the French version Petrus Dathenus a celebrated, popular preacher of the Netherlands, made a translation into Low Dutch, which appeared in 1566, and in 1568 was ordered by the Synod of Wesel to be used in all the churches for the sake of uniformity and edification. Although, subsequently other versions were made and notably a very superior one in 1580 by Philip Marnix, Lord of St. Aldegonde, yet the churches of the Netherlands continued to adhere to that of Dathenus until the latter part of the eighteenth century. It was used by the Dutch churches in the eastern part of this country until the language ceased to be used in public worship.

The Synod of Dort ordered that " only the one hundred and fifty psalms of David, the Ten Commandments, the Lord's Prayer, the twelve articles of the Christian Faith, the songs of Mary, Zacharias and Simeon versified, shall be sung in public worship. The churches are left at liberty to adopt or omit that entitled : " O thou who art our Father God ; " all others are prohibited, and where they have been already introduced they shall be discontinued as soon as possible."

By the explanatory articles adopted in this country in 1792 it is said : (Art. 65) " In the Reformed Dutch Church in America the following are approved and recommended, viz.: In the Dutch language the version of Dathenus, and the new version of psalms and hymns compiled in the Netherlands in the year 1773. In the English language the psalms and hymns compiled by Prof. Livingston, and published with the express approbation and recommendation of the General Synod in the year 1789. In the French language the psalms and hymns compiled by Theo. De Beza and Marot ; and in the German language, the psalms and hymns published at Marburgh and Amsterdam and now used in the Reformed Churches in Germany, the Netherlands and Pennsylvania."

Before this time, the church of New York had, in 1767, soon after the introduction of preaching in English, published a Psalm Book in that language, in which Brady and Tate's version, which was used in the English churches in Holland, was followed very closely, changes being made only where the music of the Dutch Psalm Book, which was retained, required it.

The book compiled by Dr. Livingston in 1789, was continued in use until 1813. By request of the General Synod, he at that time prepared a book which, besides the psalms, contained a number of hymns. Additional hymns were adopted in 1830, and also in 1846. In 1869, the book called "Hymns of the Church" was adopted, containing tunes as well as hymns; in 1871, the smaller collection known as "Hymns of Praise," and in 1879, the book called "Christian Praise" was authorized. Besides these, various books for the use of Sunday schools and prayer meetings have at different times been sanctioned.

The singing of God's praises has, not only in the Netherlands, but in America, been always regarded as the duty and privilege of the whole worshiping assembly. The choir is in theory the leader of the congregation, and not a committee with full powers to attend to that part of worship.

FEAST DAYS.

The churches in the Netherlands, and also for a long time in this country, observed the feasts of Christmas, Easter and Whitsunday, commemorative of the birth and resurrection of the Saviour, and of the outpouring of the Holy Spirit on the day of Pentecost. In addition to these, the circumcision and ascension of Christ were commemorated in many churches, and it was customary to observe the Lord's Supper on Christmas day and Easter Sunday. But the action of the various Synods clearly shows that these days were not regarded as of Divine institution, but that since they were commonly observed by the people, it was best to turn them to edification, and make them promotive of good instead of evil. The Provincial Synod held at Dordrecht in 1574 decreed (Art. 53.) : "Concerning the feast days on which, beside the Sunday, it has been customary to abstain from labor, and assemble in the church, it is resolved that we must be satisfied with the Sunday alone. However, the usual subjects on the birth of Christ may be handled in the churches on the Sunday before Christmas, and the people be admonished of the abolition of the feast-days. The same subject may also be handled on Christmas when it falls on a preaching day. It is also left to the discretion of the minister to preach on the subjects of the resurrection of Christ, and the sending of the Spirit, on Easter and Whitsunday." The Synod of Middleburg in 1581, decreed, (Art.

50) : " The congregations shall petition their magistrates that the feast-days, excepting Sunday, Christmas and Ascension, may be abolished. But in places where, by order of the magistracy, more feast-days shall continue to be observed, the minister shall endeavor, by preaching, to change unprofitable and hurtful idleness into holy and edifying exercise." The Synod held at the Hague in 1586, decreed, (Art. 60) : " The congregations shall, beside the Sunday, observe Christmas, Easter and Whitsunday, and in places where most of the feast-days, in commemoration of the benefits of Christ, as the circumcision and ascension, are by order of the magistrates observed, the minister shall endeavor, by preaching, to change the idleness of the people into holy and edifying exercise." The National Synod of Dort, 1619, decreed, (Art. 67) : " The congregation shall besides Sunday, observe Christmas, Easter, Whitsunday and the day following ; and since in most of the towns and provinces of the Netherlands, the feasts of circumcision and ascension are also observed, the minister in all places, where this is not customary, shall labor with the magistrates for the establishment of conformity with the others."

These successive decrees have been quoted so that the history of ecclesiastical action on this subject may be readily seen. It was clearly the intention at first to abolish these days entirely ; then it was thought well, since the people continued to take them for holidays, to turn them to good account by the holding of religious services ; and finally their observance was enjoined on the ground of edification. The magistrates, for reasons springing out of the circumstances of the times, and the genius and habits of the people, did not deem it expedient to abolish them, and so the Church aimed to make them promotive of piety and good morals.

She brought them to this country as a part of her institutions, and so these days were observed here just as in the Fatherland. In this country no ecclesiastical action has been taken in regard to these days, except that in explanatory article 67, (1792,) these decrees are quoted for the purpose of showing that "The Reformed Church does not believe the days usually called holy days are of Divine institution, or by preaching on those days intends anything more than to prevent evil and promote the edification of the people." References to these days do not appear at all in the constitutions of 1833 and 1874. It will be observed that saints' days were neither observed nor tolerated.

It will readily be seen that in many particulars the Reformed Churches of England and of the Netherlands assimilated. This was not strange, for the countries were closely allied; there was much intercourse between them; they were mutual helps in common troubles; they fought in the same battles for the defence of Protestantism against Spanish tyranny; they alike observed the commemorative days mentioned; used a clerical costume; received the Creeds and Liturgical forms; admitted the validity of ordination by presbyters; and the diocesan bishops of the Church of England took their seats in the Synod of Dort, with the parochial bishops of the Reformed Churches of the Netherlands and of other continental countries.*

*Rev. Mr. Vesey, the first rector of Trinity Church, in the city of New York, was inducted in office in December 1697 in the Dutch Church in Garden St. On that occasion, two Dutch clergyman, the Rev. Mr. Selyns, the pastor of the church, and the Rev. Mr. Nucella, of Kingston, assisted in the services. Mr. Vesey afterward officiated for some time in the Garden street church alternately with the Dutch clergyman until the building of Trinity Church was completed. When the Middle Dutch Church was desecrated by the British during the

Feast-days, and gowns and liturgies, the Puritans regarded as so many remnants of Popery. At Leyden the Pilgrims became uneasy because the Dutch declined to adopt their views, and they feared the influence of the surroundings there on their children. The Dutch respected their English guests, and would gladly have kept them among them, but they felt moved to seek a home in the new world, where they might have a more encouraging field for working out their cherished ideas.

The Church has always disapproved of laudatory discourses at the burial of the dead. The Synod of Dort ordered Art. 65, that "where funeral sermons are not in use they shall not be introduced, and where they have already obtained, endeavors shall be used to abolish them in the best manner possible." In explanatory Article 68, the above rule is re-affirmed, but it is added, "as it is often found to answer a good purpose to speak a word of exhortation at the time of funerals, the right of addressing the people upon such occasions is left to be exercised by every minister at his own discretion." The later revisions of the constitution make no reference to the subject of funeral services.

Rev. Dr. Livingston in 1812 published a "Funeral Service; or Meditations adapted to Funeral Addresses, being selections from Scripture." The present Liturgy contains an office for the burial of the dead.

Revolutionary War the vestry of Trinity Church passed the following resolution in 1779: "It being represented that the Old Dutch Church is now used as a hospital for his majesty's troops, this corporation impressed with a grateful remembrance of the former kindness of the members of that *ancient church* do offer the use of St. George's church to that congregation for celebrating divine worship." The courteous offer was frankly accepted—Brodhead's History, Vol. I., p. 119.

CHAPTER VIII.

GOVERNMENT AND DISCIPLINE.

The Church of God may be considered as invisible or visible. The invisible Church is composed of all the subjects of saving grace and of them exclusively, and therefore its members are known to God only. The visible is composed of outward organizations with officers, laws and ordinances, and its members are known to the world.

The question whether any particular form of Church government has been carefully defined and authoritatively enjoined by the New Testament to be of the essence of the Church we unhesitatingly answer in the negative. We have no Church constitution left by Christ or His Apostles, to be the pattern to which we must conform or forfeit our claim to the name of a Church; nor is it to be believed that there is, at the present time, a Church in existence that is precisely like the simple organizations of the early disciples.

But we have great principles announced, and the general features of Church order set forth, and also some account of officers and their functions, of discipline, and of assemblies. By the aid of these, we may form our notions of the Church government that existed in the days of the Apostles. But the fact that so little has been said on the subject in the way of command, leads us to conclude that while the general principles are unchangeable, particular forms and features may be regulated by natural prudence or Christian expediency.

Romanism takes higher ground, claiming that Christ gave to Peter authority over all the other Apostles, and over the whole Church, and that the Popes of Rome are his successors, clothed with supreme authority in the Church. Consequently, one who denies the Pope, is out of the Church, and out of the way of salvation.

High-church Episcopacy affirms that a Church constitution is established by the New Testament in conjunction with primitive tradition, requiring a threefold order in the ministry, and that if diocesan bishops, priests, and deacons in regular apostolic succession are lacking, there is no true Church of Christ.

Low-church Episcopacy on the other hand says that the Episcopal form of government is to be preferred as the best on the whole, and that it arose early in the Church ; but allows that it is not essential to the being of a Church, but that a true Church of Christ may exist under other forms.

Before the Reformation, Europe was almost completely under the dominion of Popery. For those who threw off that yoke, receiving the Gospel, and acknowledging the supreme headship of Jesus Christ, new forms of Church order became necessary. The two principal ones were the Episcopalian and Presbyterian. Independency arose afterwards as a protest against ecclesiastical tyranny and a claim for the rights of the people. The Anabaptists rose in Germany against ecclesiastical and political oppression, and unhappily ran into many excesses. The Independents of England pushed the democratic principle in the Church to the extreme, making the members of each congregation the directly governing power, and also making every congregation independent of all others.

Luther, in his Church government, forms of worship

and usages was unwilling to go further from Rome than
was necessary. He would have continued to acknowledge the Pope, if the Pope had allowed him to preach
the doctrine of justification by faith. Driven out of
the papal Church, he was compelled to provide a new
organization for his followers.

In England, Henry VIII. had no zeal for the Reformation. He at first opposed Luther; and he cast off the
authority of the Pope only when the Pope refused to
decide in accordance with his wishes that his marriage
with Catharine of Arragon, his brother's widow, was
unlawful. Although the doctrines of the Reformation spread widely among the people during his reign,
yet what is known in history as the English Reformation, was effected chiefly in the reigns of Edward VI.
and Elizabeth. After the papal reaction under Queen
Mary, the Church was settled under Queen Elizabeth.
The Sovereign is the head of the Church of England
by law established, which is Episcopal in its form of
government; which form was adopted on the ground
of expediency and political necessity rather than on
that of exclusive Divine right.

On the continent, the people ran after the word of
God and princes followed, and the people had much to
do in the matter of ecclesiastical organization. They
secured much of the popular element in their Church
constitutions, as well as of simplicity in public worship. Calvin prepared a system of ecclesiastical regulations for the Church of Geneva, and he sought for
" such as the word of God prescribes, and such as was
adopted in the early Church." This, he concluded, is
the Presbyterian system, which he accordingly established in Geneva, and which was soon carried into
France, Holland, Scotland and other countries. In the
Netherlands, the Reformation spread among the people,

but public assemblies and Synods could not be held
for some time on account of the persecuting measures
of Charles V. and Philip II. But we have reason to
believe that very early, many congregations were formed
after the Genevan model and also that conventions of
their ministers and elders were secretly held from time
to time. By the Synod of Antwerp held in 1566, the
Belgic confession of faith was adopted, whereby ministers, elders and deacons are recognized as the officers
in the Church. In 1568, a Synod of the "Churches of
the Netherlands which sit under the Cross, and are
scattered within and without the Netherlands" was
held at Wesel on the Rhine because of the troubles in
the Netherlands, and because this city was a notable
place of refuge for the persecuted adherents of the
Reformed doctrine. Of this Synod, Petrus Dathenus
was president, as we infer from the fact that his name
heads the list of subscribers to its proceedings. By
this Synod, a system of Church polity was provisionally
adopted, which is the basis of our present constitution.
Many of the nobles at first continued to adhere to the
Romish Church, though their patriotism moved them
to resist the tyranny of Spain. Many who received
the doctrines of the Reformation would, perhaps, have
preferred the Episcopal form of government; but the
people remembered how they had struggled for their
rights, and they remembered, too, how Philip had made
the hierarchy his chosen instrument for their oppression, and how he had created new bishops for the purpose of crushing their liberties. Never would they
have accepted a Church organization in which the popular, representative element was not predominant.

The articles of Church government adopted by the
Synod of Wesel in 1568, were revised by the following
Synods, viz : of Embden 1571, of Dordrecht 1574 and

1578, of Middleburg 1581, of the Hague 1586, and of Dordrecht 1619.* By all these Synods the parity of the ministry is insisted on, and the duties of elders and deacons are fully set forth. The churches in America, being until near the close of the 18th century dependent on Holland, were governed by the orders of Dort. The Coetus, which was established in 1747, was an advisory body without efficient ecclesiastical powers. The Plan of Union was adopted as a peace measure by a convention of ministers and elders held in New York in 1771, was immediately ratified by the Classis of Amsterdam, went into operation in 1772, and was gradually accepted by all the Dutch churches in the country. By this plan, the American churches agreed "to abide in all things by the constitution of the Netherlands Reformed Church as established by the ecclesiastical regulations of the Synod of Dordrecht, annis 1618 and 1619." The plan provided for the establishment of one general body, which was afterwards called a Synod, and of five particular bodies which were subsequently called Classes. The exclusive right was conferred on the General Body or Synod to admit to examinations for both licensure and ordination; the appointment of professors of Theology was determined on, and such other subjects were provided for as the circumstances demanded; and the plan was communicated to every congregation, with the hope of "an actual and hearty union into one body," which was accomplished.

In 1792, an English translation of the rules of government of the Synod of Dort was made, and this was published, accompanied by a number of articles which were framed with a particular reference to the circumstances and local situation of the churches in America.

*Kerkelyk Handboekje, Delft, 1738.

The eighty-six rules of Dort, and seventy-three explanatory articles, as they were called, were then declared to be conjointly the "ecclesiastical rule of the Dutch Reformed Church, in North America" and together they thus formed what is known as its first constitution. By one of these articles (65) authority was given to the Classes as well as the Synod to hold examinations for licensure and ordination, and this right was possessed by both Particular Synods and Classes until 1833.*

In 1815, a new edition of this constitution was published, to which was added "An appendix containing the acts and proceedings of the General Synod amending or altering any of the rules of Church government; as well as all additional rules and orders now in force." Two revisions of the constitution have since been made, one in 1833 in which the original rules of Dort and the explanatory articles were thoroughly fused together, and such changes were made, and additional rules adopted as the times and circumstances called for. By this constitution the authority to examine for licensure and ordination was taken from the Synods and confined to the Classes. The last revision was made in the year 1874.

This constitution has been established by the Church herself, not in conformity with a fancied Scriptural pattern, but on the declared ground that "for the maintenance of good order in the Church of Christ it is necessary there should be certain offices and assemblies and a strict attention to doctrines, sacraments and usages and Christian discipline."† Of all these matters the constitution treats, carefully defining the rights,

---

*Constitution of 1792.

†Introduction to the Constitution.

prerogatives and duties of the various officers and assemblies, and containing the regulations that govern and restrict each one in their exercise and practical workings. The right to authoritatively interpret the provisions of the constitution does not belong to any one of the ecclesiastical bodies, not even to the General Synod, except when an interpretation becomes necessary in deciding a case which is regularly brought before one of these bodies. Thorough loyalty to the constitution on the part of ministers, officers and members is nothing more than an honest fulfillment of a solemn contract.

OF MINISTERS OF THE WORD.

The Church has, during the greater part of its history in this country, been largely occupied with making an adequate provision for theological education, which has always been considered to be of prime importance. As the result, we now have two theological schools in this country, one at New Brunswick, New Jersey, the other at Holland, Michigan. "Every person contemplating the work of the ministry" is required to pursue his studies in one of these schools, to which he may be admitted if he has the qualifications of Church membership, Christian character and literary attainments. Having pursued the full course of prescribed studies for three years under the professors appointed by the General Synod, and having passed the final examination before the Board of Superintendents, he is furnished with a professorial certificate, which entitles him to an examination for licensure, by the Classis, to which the church of which he was a member when he began his professional studies, belongs.

But it sometimes happens that one who desires the

ministry cannot pursue the full course of study in one
of our theological schools. His age, condition in life,
or some other circumstance may make this impracticable, if not impossible, while his gifts, zeal, and promise
of usefulness may make it very desirable that a way to
the ministry should be opened to him. The way has
been opened by an exceptionally liberal and ample provision of the constitution, whereby authority is given to
the General Synod to grant dispensations from "any of
the above requirements as to study," but not from
the requirements as to examination and subscription. That is, the General Synod, may in any case,
on recommendation of a classis, shorten the course of
study; dispense with it altogether; excuse from any
particular branch of study; allow graduation from
some other theological school to be accepted in lieu of
graduation from one of our own ; allow time spent in
another school to be reckoned as if it had been spent in
one of the schools of the Synod; and even to authorize
a classis to examine and license one who has never
attended any theological school at all, but who is willing to be examined on the studies prescribed by the
constitution. A more liberal and ample provision has
not been made by any other denomination in the land,
which, at the same time, aims to maintain the general
principle of the importance to the ministry of a sound
literary and theological education. The way is opened
for one who has been graduated from any theological
seminary or from none at all, to obtain a dispensation
from the General Synod which shall entitle him to an
examination for licensure, provided only that he can
convince the Classis and the Synod that he is worthy
of such dispensation. The Classis is, not by Divine law
but by constitutional enactment, the only one of our
ecclesiastical bodies that has the right or peculiar pre-

rogative to examine for licensure; but in the exercise of this right, it, like all the other bodies, is subject to the requirements of the constitution. Accordingly any one who applies to a classis for such examination must present a professorial certificate from professors appointed by the General Synod, or proof of a dispensation granted by that Body.*

Before one can be licensed, he must, after his examination, subscribe a formula in which he declares his assent to the doctrines of the Gospel as set forth in the standards of the Church. Having been licensed, he, as a candidate for the pastoral office, preaches in churches to which the Classis may send him, or elsewhere as he may be invited; but he may not administer the sacraments, nor be a delegate to represent a church in any ecclesiastical assembly. He continues as a private member, to be subject to the discipline of the local church to which he belongs, and the Classis may for cause at any time, revoke his license to preach.

The candidate, having accepted a call, must be examined for ordination by the Classis to which the church calling him belongs; or, if he is to be ordained for missionary work, by the Classis under whose care he is at the time, as a candidate. The examination for ordination embraces a larger number of subjects than that for licensure.

The examination having been sustained, the candidate signs a formula in which he engages to preach and defend the doctrines taught in the standards, and promises that if different sentiments should afterwards arise in his mind, he will not teach them, until he shall have submitted them to the Classis for examination, and also that he will submit to the judgment of the Classis, under penalty in case of refusal, of being ipso

*Constitution Art I. Sec. 2-6

facto suspended from office. He further engages that if, at any time the Consistory or Classis shall require from him an explanation of his sentiments respecting any particular article in any one of the standards, he will be ready to comply with such request under the penalty above mentioned, reserving, however, a right to appeal from the action of the Consistory or Classis.

In ordaining ministers, the form prescribed by the Constitution is used, and the act is performed with the laying on of hands by the ministers of the Classis, and this act is never repeated in cases of subsequent installation. Before one can be installed as pastor, his name must be published to the congregation on three successive Sabbaths, so that objections to his doctrine or life, if there be any, may be presented. No person may be ordained " without settling in some congregation, except for missionary work under the direction of the Classis, or in foreign lands."

A minister may relinquish his calling only for very important reasons, about which the Classis must enquire and determine. When, by reason of age, habitual sickness, or infirmities of body or mind, he has become disqualified for the performance of ministerial duties, the Classis, on application made, and proof of such disqualification presented to them, may declare him *emeritus*, or honorably released from further service, yet retaining his title and rank as a minister. The Classis may require his congregation to pledge him such means of support, as their circumstances will warrant.

In accordance with the terms of his call, the minister engages to give himself to prayer and the ministry of the word, to dispense the sacraments, to watch over the elders and deacons, and the whole congregation; in connection with the elders to administer discipline; to catechize and instruct the youth; and in short, " by word and example always to promote the spiritual welfare of his people."

Every minister is a bishop or overseer, subordinate to none of his brethren in official rank or authority. Whatever distinctions exist in the ministry are made by position, character, attainments or fidelity.

Great care is to be exercised in the admission of a licentiate or minister from some other denomination. It is the duty of the Classis to subject him " to such examination as shall enable them to proceed with freedom in his case." Those coming from denominations who maintain doctrines different from those of the Reformed Church, are required explicitly to renounce such doctrines. Consistories of vacant congregations are cautioned against inviting ministers to preach whose character and standing are unknown to them, and they are directed, in all doubtful cases, to consult a standing committee of the Classis appointed for the purpose.

TEACHERS OF THEOLOGY.

These are taken from the ranks of the ministry, and are elected by a vote of three-fourths of the members present in the General Synod. All nominations must be made previously to the day of election ; no one may be elected on the same day on which he has been nominated, and no one nominated may be set aside except by the regular process of balloting for an election. The office can be vacated only by death, resignation, an act of discipline, or an act of the Synod declaring a professor *emeritus* on account of incapacity to perform the duties by reason of age or infirmities. Professors are directly amenable to the General Synod for their doctrine, mode of teaching and moral conduct. They are required to subscribe a formula in which they engage to teach and defend the doctrines contained in the standards ; to refute opposing errors ; to make known to the General Synod any doubts they may entertain concerning the doctrines, and to submit to the judgment of the General Synod under penalty of censure in case of refusal ; and also, to give to the Synod an explanation of their views on any point, when it shall be asked, reserving the right of a rehearing, if aggrieved.

Professors of Theology have, since 1819, not been allowed to hold pastoral charges, nor since 1833, to be members of ecclesiastical bodies, but they may preach, and administer the sacraments when invited to do so. In this respect our practice differs from that of the Presbyterian Church whose professors are members of Presbyteries and Synods, who may be appointed delegates to the General Assembly, and may hold pastoral charges. A professor intending to resign his office must give notice of his intention to the President of the General Synod three months before the next meeting of the Synod. On leaving his office, he may connect himself with such ecclesiastical judicatory as he may elect.

ELDERS.

The elders have, in connection with the ministers, the spiritual oversight of the Church. It is believed that there was in every Apostolic church a council of elders, some of whom did not preach, but only ruled in the Church. Thus we read, "let the elders that rule well, be counted worthy of double honor, especially they who labor in the word and teaching !" 1. Tim. 5 : 17.

The elders have duties to perform to the minister. If, in their judgment, he preaches unscriptural doctrine, they must call his attention to the fact, and if that avail not, they must lay the matter before the Classis.* They should kindly advise him of such faults or indiscretions in his manner of life as interfere with his usefulness. But this is not intended to encourage them in a meddlesome habit, nor to relieve them from the obligation to guard his reputation, or to defend him against the censorious or slanderous. If he is charged with conduct that would make his appearance in the pulpit offensive, they may forbid him to officiate, pending an investigation by the Classis, which investigation is to be demanded. The elders should sympathize and co-operate with the minister in work for the advancement of the Redeemer's Kingdom, giving, not cold assent, but zealous assistance to his endeavors.

They have duties to the Church. They, in connection with the minister, admit persons to the sacraments, and have the oversight of all who are admitted. They instruct, admonish or comfort, as the case may require. They should tenderly warn the negligent, admonish backsliders, heal divisions, and by the various methods of Christian discipline endeavor to save the erring. It is enjoined on them to visit the families in the congregation, and before every administration of the Lord's Supper, they are solemnly asked whether they know of any communicant who has walked unworthily, so that all cases requiring it may be attended to. The Synod of Wesel directed that every congregation should be divided into as many districts as there were elders, and that each elder should have charge of a district. The elders made their reports of the condition of the congregation at the preparatory service, and cases requiring the exercise of discipline

---

*The giving of the hand by the Elders to the Minister after service, signifies approbation of the doctrine preached, and the withholding is expressive of dissent from it.

were thus brought before the Consistory. Elders are also sent as delegates to the Classes and Synods, in which the deacons never appear.

DEACONS.

The account of the appointment of the first deacons we have in the 6th chapter of the Acts. The Apostles being unable to give proper attention to the wants of the poor, seven men were appointed for that business, and they were called deacons, that is, servants or attendants. To the deacon as such belongs, not the ministration of the word, which pertains to the minister, nor the government of the Church which is the function of the elder, but the care of the poor. He collects and distributes the alms, searches out the needy, and ministers to their necessities. The poor members of the church in which the alms have been collected, have the preference in the distribution. After them, the wants of other poor saints or strangers may be supplied. Since provision by law or otherwise has, in our time, been made by every community for the care of the poor, and various societies and institutions for mutual aid have been multiplied, this office has not maintained its ancient importance. Still it is acknowledged throughout our communion, and indeed in all Christian Churches, that every church should care for its indigent members. The churches of Holland have always been famed for their liberal provision for the needy. There have been times when more was contributed by these churches for the sustenance of persecuted refugees than for their own expenses.

ELECTION OF ELDERS AND DEACONS.

In establishing a new church, the elders and deacons, are chosen by the male communicants uniting in its organization. In established churches, the communicants may choose from a double number nominated by the Consistory, or they may nominate and elect independently of the Consistory, or the Consistory itself may choose the successors of those whose terms of office are about to expire. The names of the persons elected must be published to the congregation on three successive Sabbaths for the concurrent approbation of the congregation, or the presentation of objections, if any exist. A church which has for years practised any one of these methods, may not abandon it for another, without the permission of the Classis.

LIMITATION OF THE TERM OF OFFICE.

The elders and deacons are chosen for a limited term of two years. In every year, the terms of one-half of the members of the Consistory expire, but an immediate re-election is lawful, if it be thought advisable. The feature of limited terms was taken from Calvin's ordinances and adopted by the Synod of Wesel in 1568, and has from that time been adhered to by the churches in the Netherlands and in America. In the Presbyterian churches of America, the elders have, until quite recently, been invariably chosen for life; but in many of them, the principle of a limited term is now acted upon. The following are among some of the advantages of this plan.

1. It affords relief. Sometimes the duties of these officers press heavily and become burdensome, especially to a man who duly appreciates them and is obliged at the same time to be diligent in his worldly business. Many a one would cheerfully serve for one term occasionally, who could not well afford to do it permanently.

2. It affords an opportunity for securing the services of men of wisdom, experience and influence who have been received from other churches, and also of young

men of energy and special promise who have grown up in the church. Places that become regularly vacant may thus be filled with desirable men who could not otherwise be obtained without an enlargement of the Consistory. Such enlargement may often be made in growing churches to great advantage, for thereby tried and useful officers may be retained, and at the same time others who are well-qualified, secured. It is in any case wise to retain a valuable elder or deacon, and not to fill a vacancy with an inefficient one for the sake of maintaining the principle of rotation.

3. It is calculated to give to the largest number an interest in, and familiarity with church matters, and so the intelligent service of many members is obtained. The worth of many a private member has been little known until he was placed by the church in a responsible station, for true worth is ever modest and retiring.

4. It may happen that a man is in office of whom it is desirable to get rid in the easiest way possible. If he were guilty of heresy or immorality, the mode of procedure would be plain, but usually charges cannot be formulated. The man when elected may have been unexceptionable, but events have since occurred that have impaired his usefulness. Perhaps he is a man of piety, but weak-minded or vain-glorious, arbitrary or obstinate, or by reason of some mental obliquity, or unhappy temper, an unpleasant and inefficient church officer, and whose influence is damaging rather than helpful. What can you do with him if he is chosen for life, and he can not be removed by discipline? It may be said that he should resign, and should be advised to do so, if he does it not of his own accord. This is well, but who does not know that the men who ought to resign, are not aware of it, and usually decline advice to do so. By our mode, they are silently dropped and

fall back to places among the private members of the church. Yet elders and deacons going out of the present acting Consistory do not lose every function of office, for the elder though not in the Consistory may sit as a delegate in the Classis or the Synods. Besides, when very important matters are before the church, the great Consistory may be called, which is composed of all who have ever been elders and deacons, and which has advisory power that is usually respected by the acting Consistory. The limited term of office belonged to Calvin's system at Geneva, where elders were elected annually.* It has always been practised by the Protestant Church of France, as it was also by the Church of Scotland in its early history. Rev. Dr. Samuel Miller, late professor in Princeton Theological Seminary, admits that there is no infringement on the Presbyterian principle in annual elections. "Where a church," says he, "is large, containing a sufficient number of grave, pious, and prudent members to furnish an advantageous rotation, and where the duties of the office are many and arduous, it may not be without its advantages to keep up some change of incumbency in this office.

Undoubtedly, the chief aim should be to secure the best men attainable for church officers, and to take advantage of the principle of rotation to gain that end; but not to change if it must be for the worse. Better, as has been said, re-elect a good man, than put an objectionable one into his place. It is thought by some that every male member is entitled to his turn in office and has a right to expect an election in due time; but this is no more reasonable than that every good citizen may look for his turn to be elected to the Legislature or to Congress.

*Henry's Life of Calvin, Vol. I., p. 385
†Essay on Ruling Elders, pp. 276-8.

OF ECCLESIASTICAL ASSEMBLIES.

THE CONSISTORY.

A local church is organized by the formation of a Consistory which is done by the Classis. The term Consistory was formerly applied to the body composed of the minister and elders, while the deacons formed a separate board. But in America, the minister, elders and deacons have always been united in one board, and have possessed certain joint powers in addition to their separate, peculiar functions. In admitting persons to the sacraments, in exercising discipline, and in choosing delegates to the Classis, the elders with the minister alone have a voice, while to the deacons belongs officially the care of the poor.

"When joined together in one board, the elders and deacons have all an equal voice in whatever relates to the temporalities of the church, to the calling of a minister, or the choice of their own successors, in all which they are considered the general and joint representatives of the people."*

In our churches, at least in the states of New York and New Jersey with rare exceptions, the Consistory is the legal corporation, the members of which are, by law, authorized as trustees to manage the temporalities of the church. The churches of other denominations usually have Boards of Trustees separate from the church officers, and who often are not church members, in whom the title of the property is vested, and who have entire control of the temporalities.

This feature of our polity is calculated to prevent a clashing of interests, and disputes about preroga-

*Constitution, Art. 6, sec. 2.

tive, and is a testimony in favor of a Christian as against a carnal, worldly policy in the management of the temporalities. It may not be denied, however, that the consideration of the temporalities is apt to consume an undue proportion of time in meetings of the Consistory. Yet, the advantage of giving men who pretend not to piety, a controlling influence in church affairs and of securing the aid of shrewd calculators and managers may be very dearly bought. Moreover, temporal and spiritual interests in a church are more closely connected than men usually suppose, so that it seems to be desirable that the same persons should preside over both, and especially if the people are fairly represented.

This feature in our polity existed in our churches in America from the earliest period of their history. In 1784, the Legislature of the state of New York passed an act directing the churches of all denominations to elect Boards of Trustees for the management of the temporalities. These were to be separate from the spiritual officers and one-third of the members were annually to go out of office. Vigorous efforts were made at once by the members of the Dutch Church under the lead of the Rev. Dr. Livingston to procure the passage of a clause in the act, which should allow her to maintain her long-established practice. The Legislature finally assented, and enacted that the ministers, elders and deacons elected according to the rules and usages of the Reformed Dutch churches within the state shall be the trustees for every such church or congregation.* The law in New Jersey is similar to this, and perhaps the same is true of other states. The elders may and should meet separately for the con-

---

*Gunn's life of Livingston, 1st ed. p. 287.

sideration of the spiritual matters that pertain to their office, such as receiving members by confession of faith or certificate, dismissing them to other churches, and attending to church discipline. The names of members received must be published to the congregation and registered. When members remove without the bounds of the congregation they are enjoined to procure certificates of dismission.

The right to call a minister is lodged in the acting Consistory embracing the deacons as well as elders, but they are enjoined to ascertain the choice of the people by consulting the Great Consistory, or in such other way as they may deem best. Happily, the hazardous method of a public congregational meeting is not enjoined.

When a call is to be made, a minister of the Classis must be present to superintend the proceedings and report to the Classis. The call is the contract between pastor and people, and it defines their duties and mutual engagements. The general form of the call is prescribed by the constitution, while particulars as to salary and specific duties to suit the case are inserted. A call should always be read to the congregation for their information. It must be approved by the Classis before it can be placed in the hands of the person called. The plan of stated supplies and annual contracts has always been discouraged in our Church, on the ground that it puts the minister in the position of a hireling, and the union of minister and people is liable to be broken at any moment by caprice or passion.

THE CLASSIS.

The Classis corresponds to the Presbytery of the Presbyterian Church. It is composed of a number of ministers and of delegated elders from such churches as have by the Particular Synod been joined together in a Classis. A Classis cannot be constituted with less than three ministers and three elders. Stated meetings are held twice a year.

The Classis examines students for licensure and candidates for ordination, approves calls, constitutes and dissolves pastoral relations, ordains, installs, suspends, dismisses and deposes ministers, organizes and disbands churches, approves of and dissolves combinations of congregations, exercises a general supervisory power over consistories, and is a court of appeal from the acts of the Consistory in judicial cases.

The Classis keeps a book of subscriptions of candidates and ministers, and annually reports to the Particular Synod the names of all who have been licensed or ordained during the year, as well as all pastoral changes. For the classical visitations formerly made to the churches by committees to enquire into their condition, and to ascertain whether all parties were fulfilling their obligations, the constitution of 1833 substituted the following questions, with the exception of the seventh, which has since been added, and which are to be answered by every pastor and elder at the spring meeting of the Classis :

1st. Are the doctrines of the Gospel preached in your congregation in their purity, agreeably to the Word of God, the confession of faith, and the catechisms of our Church ?

2nd. Is the Heidelberg Catechism regularly explained agreeably to the constitution of the Reformed (Dutch) Church ?

3rd. Are the catechizing of the children and the instruction of the youth faithfully attended to ?

4th. Is family visitation faithfully performed ?

5th. Is the 5th sec. 6th Art. in the constitution of our Church, relating to the conduct of church members, carefully obeyed, previous to each communion ?

6th. Is the temporal contract between ministers and people fulfilled in your congregation ?

7th. Is a contribution made annually by your congregation to each of the benevolent boards and funds of the Church ?

THE PARTICULAR SYNOD.

There are four Particular Synods, viz: of New York, of Albany, of Chicago, and of New Brunswick. These differ in one respect from the Synods of the Presbyterian Church, in that they are delegated bodies; each one consisting of four ministers and four elders from each Classis belonging to the Synod, while the Presbyterian Synods are constituted of all the ministers within a certain district, and an elder from every church in that district.

The Particular Synod has the power to form new classes, and to transfer congregations from one classis to another, has a general superintendence over the spiritual interests of the Classes, and is a court of appeal from the decisions of the Classes in cases of discipline. Its decisions are final in cases which have originated in the Consistory, with the exception of such as are deemed by a certain number of members to be of sufficient importance to be carried to the General Synod. The Synod meets annually, receives the reports of the Classes, from which it prepares a report to the General Synod, accompanied with the statistical tables of the Classes.

THE GENERAL SYNOD.

The General Synod is composed of three ministers and three elders from each of the Classes embracing fifteen or less than fifteen churches, and an additional representation of one minister and one elder for each additional five churches. These delegates are nominated by the Classes and confirmed by the Particular Synods. The General Synod meets annually on the first Wednesday in June, and usually remains about ten days in session.

This body has entire control of the theological schools. It constitutes Particular Synods and makes changes in them. It is the channel of friendly correspondence with the highest judicatories of other denominations, for the purpose of promoting union and concert in measures for the maintenance of sound doctrine, and the promotion of the cause of religion and piety. The various boards are agencies created by the General Synod and are directly responsible to it. It has a general superintendence over the spiritual concerns of the whole Church, and is the final court of appeal in judicial cases excepting such as have been finally decided by the Particular Synod.'

It is worthy of notice that in this form of government there is a lay representation throughout. In the Consistory there are usually eight laymen to one minister; in the Classis there is intended to be an equal number of ministers and elders, though ministers without charge sometimes give the ministers the preponderance and sometimes vacant congregations give it to the elders. To the Synods, an equal number of clerical and lay delegates is always appointed.

OF DISCIPLINE.

"Discipline is the exercise of the authority which the Lord Jesus Christ has given to His Church." The term is sometimes used in a wide sense to embrace all that belongs to government. More frequently it is used in a narrower sense to describe the treatment of offending members.

The objects of discipline are, "the removal of offences; the vindication of the honor of Christ; the promotion of purity, and the general edification of the Church; and also the benefit of the offender." Particular attention is called to the last-mentioned object, because an act of discipline is thought by many to be an act of persecution, an interference with personal liberty, a contest for victory between two parties, and that unholy elements belong to it unavoidably. Rarely is it understood that Church courts are more disposed to neglect discipline than to enforce it, and that when compelled to act, they do so in sorrow, and always with a view not of casting any one out of the church, but of saving the soul, and through penitence and confession to retain the erring in the church. Discipline is intended for salvation and not for destruction. But the friends of one who has been placed under discipline, not understanding this, are apt to find fault with the church authorities, and instead of thanking them for their faithfulness, and co-operating with them in endeavors to save one whom they love, they do all in their power to thwart these beneficent efforts, sometimes even forming parties and combinations for that purpose.

Great care, prudence and tenderness are required for this work, lest we pluck up the wheat with the tares. Many in the Church are so thoroughly worldly, that we cannot but doubt their gracious state, and yet they art not subjects for judicial process, for they do not hold erroneous doctrines, neglect ordinances, nor commit scandalous sins. A wide margin must also be left for the decisions of conscience on matters about which the Word of God is silent. Another man's conscience may allow what mine condemns, and he is not to be judged by my conscience. "Nothing," says the constitution, "shall be admitted as matter of accusation or considered an offence which cannot be proved to be such from Scripture, or the regulations of the Church founded on Scripture."

Offences are divided into two classes, private and public. "A private offence is one that is known to an individual only, or to very few." The course of procedure in such a case is laid down by the Saviour in the eighteenth chapter of Matthew. An offended person may not noise abroad his grievance, nor betake himself to the Consistory, nor keep silent and cherish a grudge in his heart, nor even wait for the offender to come and make acknowledgment, though it is his duty to do so. He must go to the offender and tell him his fault without a witness present. If this fail, he must take one or two witnesses with him. Not until all such private efforts have failed, may he appeal to the church authorities. If having neglected them, he brings the matter before the church, he is liable to censure for so doing.

Public offences are such as are so notorious and scandalous that no private measures could obviate their evil effects. The Consistory is, in such cases, bound to act without waiting for some individual to bring an accusation. A minister thus charged cannot be brought to trial by his Consistory, but they can, as a prudent interference, forbid him to officiate until the Classis shall have investigated the case. Elders, deacons, and private members are amenable to the Consistory.

At every meeting of the Consistory held immediately before the celebration of the Lord's Supper, the elders are solemnly asked whether they know of any one who has walked unworthily, or departed from the Christian profession. Would it not be well at such meetings always to read over the list of communicants, so that every elder might have some knowledge of every communicant? Would it not be well, also, for every elder to possess such a list in print or manuscript to examine at his leisure, and in which required changes might from time to time be made?

In answer to the inquiry referred to, the names are mentioned of those who are becoming negligent in their walk, and committees are appointed to visit, and to kindly admonish them. Sometimes cases are reported that are so serious that the Consistory is compelled to table charges for trial. The accused is cited to appear, is furnished with a copy of the charges, and allowed ten days, at least, to put in his answer. If he refuse to appear, he is cited a second time, and warned that if he again refuse, he will not only be liable to censure for contumacy, but that the trial will proceed as if he were present.

The testimony of more than one witness is required to establish a charge. Witnesses who cannot be brought before a court may be examined by commission. All witnesses may be cross-examined, their testimony must be faithfully recorded, and copies given to the parties if desired. Accusations brought more than two years after the time when the offence is alleged to have been committed, will not be admitted, unless good reason for the delay be shown. No professional counsel may plead in any of the ecclesiastical courts; but a member of the court may conduct a case for the accused, and a member of Classis may be engaged to conduct a case on either side before a Consistory.

There are three forms of punishment: First, for the lightest offences, admonition; second, for the more gross, and especially public offences and for contempt of admonitions, suspension from the Lord's table; third, excommunication. The sentence of suspension may be published to the congregation or not, at the discretion of the Consistory. The suspended member must not be treated as one cut off, but be frequently admonished and encouraged to repentance, and prayed for, and restored with joy if he gives evidence of penitence. But if, after repeated admonitions, he remains incorrigible, the third and last measure may be resorted to, viz : excommunication. This, however, may be done only with the advice of the Classis, and several steps are necessary. In the first place, the whole history of the case, without mention of the name of the offender, must be publicly given to the congregation, and they be exhorted to pray for him. In the second place, the same thing is to be done, with mention of the name. In the third place, the congregation is informed that unless the offender repent, he shall be excommunicated. Thus their tacit approbation is secured, and the way prepared for the final act, the reading of the form provided for excommunication.

If the excommunicated person becomes penitent, and desires re-admission, it is publicly declared to the congregation, and if no objections are presented, he is publicly re-admitted, according to the form appointed for that purpose.

All human tribunals are fallible, and injustice may be done to a man by a Church court. A system of appeals from the lower to the higher judicatories has therefore been established, with a view of securing the ends of justice, and of furnishing one who is aggrieved by a sentence with every facility for obtaining a reversal of judgment. The Particular Synod is the final court of appeal for all cases originating in the Consistory, except such as may, by a certain number of the members of the Synod, be declared to be proper ones to be carried up to the General Synod. A complaint may be made by a minority of a judicatory, to the next higher body, of the action of the majority. In such cases, there is no personal grievance, but a conviction that the action is a violation of the constitution, or in some other way contrary to the interests of truth or godliness. The method of procedure is the same in case of a complaint as of an appeal.

It is to be regretted that consistories so often neglect to notice cases of departure from a Christian profession until they are compelled by public opinion to do it, and then it is often too late to accomplish any thing but strife and division. The work would be far more easy and satisfactory, and occasion for it far less frequent, if they were careful to mark the first steps of inconsistency in a member, and kindly to warn him at once.

Not seldom is the notion entertained by Church members that they can discipline themselves, or dismiss themselves to the world, or drop silently out of the church. They will tell us that they once belonged to a certain church, and on questioning them, we learn that their connection with it has not been broken by discipline, nor by dismission to another church. They have only removed from within the bounds of that church, or if they continue to live within them, have ceased to attend public worship, and to partake of the Lord's Supper, and they consider that they have thus been released from the vows that once rested on them. Great would be their astonishment if called to account by the Consistory, and yet to this they are clearly liable; for how can membership be destroyed by a violation of the obligations connected with it? How can a man get out of the church, unless by death, without the knowledge of, or some act on the part of the church?

Members, likewise, who have removed within the bounds of another church, without taking letters of dismission, and who have neglected ordinances, are sometimes received by Consistories on confession of faith, as if they came directly from the world. If this be a regular procedure, then a person may be a member of two churches at the same time. It is proper for such persons to make confession of their fault to the church to which they belong, and be reconciled to it, so that they may receive a letter of dismission to the church with which they desire to be connected.

The proper and careful exercise of discipline has much to do with the life, prosperity and efficiency of the Church. When offenders are faithfully dealt with according to the directions of Holy Scripture, the Church appears "fair as the moon, clear as the sun, and terrible as an army with banners."

CHAPTER IX.

CONCLUSION.

In the foregoing history, great, but not undue prominence has been given to the serious obstacles to the growth of the Church that existed almost to the close of the last century. That she has, since their removal, made the advance she should have done no one will claim. Ground has undoubtedly been lost in some places, especially in our large cities, and in many places churches might have been established at an earlier day. Still there has been a steady, healthy growth, as the following statistics show :

In 1784, there were 82 churches and 30 ministers ; in 1815, there were 130 churches and 80 ministers ; in 1855, there were 364 churches and 348 ministers ; in 1888, there were 546 churches and 555 ministers. It thus appears that one-third of the whole number of churches have been organized, and one-third of the ministers added during the last 33 years.

Losses which, however, were not very serious have been suffered by means of two local secessions, during the present century. Of the former, Rev. Dr. Solomon Froeligh, one of the Professors of Theology, appointed in 1797, and a man of eminent theological attainments, was the leader. Having made himself liable to censure by acts of aggression on a neighboring church, he preferred to secede rather than to confess his fault, make amends, and submit to the Church authorities. He went out in 1822, taking with him his two congregations of Hackensack and Schraalenberg. Four suspended

ministers with their elders and portions of their
churches joined him in the movement, and formed
"The True Reformed Dutch Church in the United
States of America." This number was increased by
accessions so that in 1824, 16 Churches and 10 ministers were reported. They gave as reasons for their
withdrawal, the prevalence of doctrinal errors, and
singularly enough, the neglect of discipline in the
Reformed Dutch Church. They retain all the doctrinal
standards and liturgical forms. They are a people
by themselves holding no fellowship with other denominations, and declining to co-operate in Bible, tract or
missionary effort. Their churches, at the present
time 13 in number are, for the most part small,
feeble and struggling to maintain an existence, with
the exception of a few in northern New Jersey. This
division caused, for a long time, bitter strife in the localities to which it was confined.*

The latter secession took place among the Holland
ministers and churches of the Particular Synod of
Chicago in 1882 and was caused by the refusal of the
General Synod to denounce Free-masonry, or to declare
that one's connection with a masonic lodge was good
cause for and demanded the exercise of Church discipline. A few ministers and churches and parts of
churches, for this cause withdrew from the Reformed
Church and joined themselves to an already existing body called "The Holland Christian Reformed
Church."

The review of the past is of little profit unless we are
prepared by it for the work before us. If mistakes have
been made, the lessons taught by them may be despised
only at our peril. The Reformed (Dutch) Church in

---

*Brinkerhoff's History of the True Reformed Dutch Church.

America must do her part for the advancement of the Redeemer's Kingdom. So long as she maintains her separate organization and distinctive character, she must not only hold her ground, but vigorously carry on the work of extension, or she will be disintegrated and her churches will be absorbed by the surrounding large denominations. The historical associations of centuries, the church attachments that have come down from generation to generation, make many shrink from the thought that she should cease to be known in this land. There are also those who fear that her absorption would result in so much loss to the cause of the Redeemer; and who claim that she has peculiar facilities for working in some fields; that she can do more for the cause of Christ by retaining her separate organization than by a fusion with some Church of similar faith and order; and that she has enough of a distinctive character to justify the continuance of her denominational existence. Whenever it shall be clearly indicated that it is her Lord's will that her denominational existence should cease, may she have grace promptly and cheerfully to acquiesce. Meanwhile let her be found faithful in working in her own sphere and with her own agencies for the prosperity and extension of the Kingdom of her Lord.

Are there any peculiar difficulties in the way of her work and of her extension?

Is there anything objectionable in her doctrine? So far from it, we believe that her faith is eminently Scriptural, and that it commends itself to all Evangelical Christians and especially so much of it as is contained in her catechisms, the teaching of which is enjoined.

Is her government defective? It rather seems to combine admirably, the conservative and popular elements, and when understood is generally approved.

Is there anything objectionable in her worship? On the contrary she has adopted the mean between the two extremes of naked simplicity and showy ritual; between rigid prescription and perfect liberty. She has her prescribed order of worship; and also forms which must be used on certain occasions, while within these limits considerable liberty is allowed in ordinary worship.

Is her policy contracted? She has organized her institutions and agencies with a view to extension as well as to the maintenance of ground possessed. She took her place at once with the other denominations in the work of missions, foreign and domestic. At no time has she displayed more interest and zeal in this work than at the present day. Perhaps her movements are not as rapid as are those of some other Churches, perhaps not as rapid as they should be; but they are in the right direction, and prompted by confidence in a thorough proclamation of the Gospel as the only regenerator of mankind.

Is her spirit illiberal? Entirely and emphatically the contrary. The Church in Holland was remarkable for her tolerant and liberal spirit. She welcomed and provided for persecuted Scotch, English, French, German and Italian Protestants. The Church in this country has always lived in peace and maintained friendly intercourse with her neighbors. She met the Episcopal Church of England with Christian courtesy when brought to New Amsterdam, and gave her the use of her own building for worship. She has cordially received into her communion the ministers and members of other denominations and given them honor. Some of our most eminent and devoted ministers have been thus received, and of private members none are more warmly attached to the Church and her institutions than many who are in the Church, from intelligent choice, and without prejudices of birth and early association. We have congregations composed of members, who, for the most part, are not of Holland descent, but who have studied the Church, and have chosen her to be their ecclesiastical home.

Our people are material that can be readily worked into any sound Christian denomination. Led by providential circumstances or convictions of duty into other Churches, they become at once as loyal and zealous as any. Prominent in the ranks of other denominations, you will find many who, in infancy, received the baptismal seal in the Reformed (Dutch) Church. They seldom return to their mother Church when opportunity offers, for they love not change. It is not to their discredit that they thus fully identify themselves with the Churches in which God has in His providence placed them. Perhaps motives less worthy than these mentioned, have sometimes led men to pass from the Church of their fathers to some other denomination.

It has been contended that her name as the Dutch Church has been through almost her whole history, a mighty hindrance to her progress. Of the two oldest, and for a long time strongest Churches in New York, the one came from the Netherlands and used the Dutch language, the other from England and used the English tongue. The one was popularly known as the Dutch Church, the other as the English. When these Churches became independently organized in this country, the latter placed the word " Episcopal " in her title to indicate her form of government; the former placed the word " Dutch " in her title to indicate her nationality. She was in government Presbyterian, but could not take that name because it had been already appropriated by another denomination. She could not derive a distinctive name from her doctrines, for they were substantially the same as those of the Episcopal, Presbyterian and Congregational Churches. She very naturally, having no prophetic eye to see what this country was to be, and what it would demand of her, adopted the name by which she was already popularly known and which indicated her origin and language, and which was suitable for the time. If the word Dutch has in times past been a hindrance, it is so no longer, since it has been removed from the title.

In the course of time, as the country developed and the Dutch language fell into disuse, many began to feel that a great and unfortunate mistake had been made by placing in the title of the Church a word indicative of a foreign origin and a foreign language. It was claimed that, through unavoidable misunderstandings, this name could not but be a serious obstacle to the prosperity of the denomination, and to its growth in new States and Territories. But no formal attempt was made for the removal of this presumed obstacle until the year 1866, when the General Synod appointed a committee to consider the propriety and expediency of eliminating the word Dutch from the title of the Church. The committee reported to the next Synod in favor of such elimination, and the Synod, having approved the report of the committee, recommended the proposed change to the favorable consideration of the Classes. A large majority of the Classes having approved of the change, the General Synod in November, 1867, declared the proposed amendment to be from that time a part of the constitution, and .that the Church should thenceforth be known as the Reformed Church in America; ordering, at the same time, that wherever the word Dutch occurs in the constitution it should be retained, to prevent all doubt or dispute in regard to the continued identity of the Church ; but that it should be enclosed in brackets, to " indicate the purpose of the Church to discourage the ecclesiastical and popular use of the word as part of the name." *

It is an interesting fact that about the same time the word German was removed from the title of the German Reformed Church, which body is now known as the Reformed Church in the United States.

A more extensive and thorough acquaintance with the history and characteristics of the Reformed (Dutch) Church would, we believe, increase the loyalty of her members, and so contribute greatly to her efficiency. Of this we have been too neglectful. We have read the histories of other denominations and neglected our own. We have joined with others in praise of their God-fearing, heroic ancestors, and have not even inquired whether our own were worthy of remembrance. Our youth have not been allowed to remain in ignorance of the Pilgrims, of the Mayflower and Plymouth Rock, while they have learned little about the glorious and protracted contest of the Dutch for civil and religious liberty. The present generation is rapidly correcting the error of the past. Our best historians have brought Dutch heroes, statesmen and divines to the front, and the record of their characters and deeds has awakened enthusiasm. It is now well known that no shame can come to a member of the Reformed (Dutch) Church from ancestral associations.

Let her distinctive characteristics be recognized, and her distinctive customs and usages be respected. Her doctrines, her polity and forms are open to all for examination ; and her own ministers and members, at least, should make themselves familiar with them.

*Acts and Proceedings of the General Synod. Vol. XI., p. 334.

While no one advocates a reproduction in all particulars of the Church of 200 years ago, it may yet be asked, whether the state of society has changed so much as to make all her ancient customs impracticable or even inexpedient at the present time. Why cannot her former singularly faithful care in catechizing and training the young under pastoral supervision be now exercised? Why cannot the eldership now be as efficient as it was when every elder had his particular district to watch over, and whose condition he was to report to the Consistory? Why cannot the family visitations be, to a very considerable extent, at least, made as in former times? Why cannot the congregation unite in singing the high praises of God? Why cannot the forms which are prescribed be used in their integrity? Why cannot the Heidelberg catechism be expounded as required by the constitution, and so as both to edify and interest the people? Why cannot the salutation be given, and the commandments and creed be read, and the Lord's Prayer offered every Lord's day in public worship? Why cannot the elders and deacons observe the old and appropriate custom of occupying official seats in the congregation? Why should not a deacon wait upon the minister in the administration of baptism, and why should not the deacons carry the bread and wine to the communicants in the administration of the Lord's Supper, it being their appropriate work? In carrying our Church into new localities we gain nothing, but lose much, by attempting to hide her peculiarities and by taking pains to show that she is in no wise different from some other well-known denomination. The question very justly presents itself, why, if you in no respect differ from your neighbor, do you maintain a separate existence, and look for perpetuation?

Her institutions should receive the cordial and liberal support of her members. Those established for academic, collegiate and theological education have special claims on our young men, apart from the fact that they are prepared to do their work as well as any similar institutions in the land. The missionary, education, and other boards have special claims on the members of the Church. Their regular and liberal support is no proof of sectarian narrowness, nor does it interfere with a hearty co-operation with other Christians in the various noble institutions of benevolence, in which they are so pleasantly and efficiently united.

Children should be consecrated to, and trained for Christ, to serve Him in the various callings of life, and especially in the sacred ministry, for ministers are greatly needed for the supply of new and vacant congregations, as well as for the foreign field. It is a sad fact that we are often obliged to resort to other denominations for men to supply our deficiency. Let Christian parents consider this, and pray God to honor them by making their sons ambassadors of the Lord Jesus Christ.

Property should be laid at the feet of the Redeemer. The Church, in order to work, and to extend herself, needs money as well as men. She must know that the gold and silver are the Lord's. The Spirit of the Lord is working a mighty revolution on this subject. May it go on until it shall be complete. Self-seeking and avarice cannot stand before the two-edged sword of God's truth, wielded by the omnipotent Spirit.

While we thank God for our heritage, let us cultivate the liberal spirit of which our Church has always been so illustrious an example, and let us greet all who are of the household of faith as brethren. Above all, let us seek membership in the true Church, the

company of the redeemed, gathered from among all
communions and peoples. that glorious Church, which
will appear hereafter, without spot or wrinkle or any
such thing; remembering that we cannot enter heaven
as members of the Reformed (Dutch) Church, but only
as sinners saved by grace.

INDEX.

www.ingramcontent.com/pod-product-compliance
Lightning Source LLC
Chambersburg PA
CBHW030733280326
41926CB00086B/1261